The Intimate Marriage

For engaged and married couples who desire
increased intimacy in their relationship
with God and with one another

by David and Linda Roeder

Foreword by
Pastor Ronald L. Peake

Unless noted, all Scripture quotations are from the King James Version of the Bible.
Scripture quotations marked PNT are from the Power New Testament.
Copyright ©1996, William J. Morford. Used by permission.

Art, cover, Edith Roeder
Art, dedication, Paula Peake
Caricatures, Michael Peake
Editors, Michael and Jennifer Blasi

All rights reserved. No part of this publication may be reproduced, stored in a retrieval system, or transmitted by any means – electronic, mechanical, photographic (photocopying), recording, or otherwise – without prior permission in writing from the author.

"Intimate Marriage", a workbook for use during ministry sessions, or as a self-study workbook for engaged or married couples.

International Standard Book Number: : 978-1489533197

- ☐ "Ministry Manual For Biblical Marriage Preparation and Marriage Ministry"
  Copyright © Paraklesis Ministries, 2013
- ☐ "upRIGHTing RELATIONSHIPS" by Linda L. Roeder. Inspiring truths from God's Word that designed to transform your heart and your relationships.
- ☐ "Relationship". A workbook for individuals or groups who desire greater intimacy with God and a stronger relationship with others. (e.g.: choose this workbook for families, staff, church or business groups, Bible studies, youth groups, or a married person whose spouse will not be completing a workbook with them.)
- ☐ "Bible College course on Biblical Marriage Counseling". For personal study. "Counselor's Manual" is the companion text.
- ☐ "Principles of Practice". (Straw man) This manual will assist those who are developing policies for their counseling or lay ministry.
- ☐ "Transformational Apostolic and Prophetic Living Workbook" How to live in godly, vibrant, healthy personal relationships, marriages, and families so that you can…Impact, Influence, and Inspire others in their relationships with God and others!

To contact us or to order products:
Paraklesis Ministries
c/o Christian International Central
2377 E. Country Road 250 South
Versailles, IN 47042-9798
(812) 689-5503
Email: dcroeder@gmail.com

Website: www.dave-linda.com

DEDICATION

This workbook is dedicated to our Lord

Wonderful…

Counselor…

Mighty God …

Prince of Peace …

Adapted from Isaiah 9:6

APPRECIATION

When we first asked the Lord into our hearts, our pastor and his wife compassionately taught us God's plan for marriage. Much of what you read in this workbook is the fruit of their love for us.

Our initial ministry as a couple began when we were graciously given an opportunity to work with the wonderful high school group at our church. We "grew up" with those kids! Their love for the Lord, their zeal, and their desire to serve Him were extraordinary.

We graduated from the high school ministry to the "young couples" ministry at about the time that many of them were getting married, and they humbly received from us as we began to do marriage preparation ministry. We will always treasure the times we have been privileged to spend with these young people, honing our ministry skills and our own marriage at the same time.

"But that on the good ground are they, which in an honest and good heart, having heard the word, keep it, and bring forth fruit with patience." Luke 8:15

FOREWARD

Dave and Linda Roeder are well qualified to write this workbook. They qualify for this work by having a marriage that is a model for others. In addition, the book grows out of several years of pre-marriage ministry with the young couples of our church. That period of ministry was wonderfully successful in the lives of these young adults. The situations they have encountered, the successes and the difficulties that occurred during that time, have been valuable learning tools. That wisdom has been incorporated into the <u>Ministry Manual for Biblical Marriage Preparation and Marriage Ministry</u> and this companion workbook, <u>The Intimate Marriage.</u> They have also written "Relationship", a workbook for individuals, families, and groups.

These resources address a great need in the Body of Christ. As a pastor for seventeen years, I have often looked for a workbook to use as a resource and guide for marriage and pre-marriage ministry. Of the many that are available, this is the best and most practical that I have seen. It's simplicity and ease of use sets it apart. It does not preach and instruct, but rather sets up an environment in which people can seek and hear from God about the needs and issues of their life. This manual leads the users to seek God and to hear from God for themselves. It is the seeking of Him that leads to the personal revelations that form the most significant and lasting changes in our lives. This manual will change the lives of all those who use it.

Ronald L. Peake
Pastor
Agape Fellowship Ministries

BIBLIOGRAPHY

Fichtner, John, Marriage Course, Liberty Church, Marrietta, Georgia, 1991.

Friend, Joseph H. and David B. Guralnik (ed.), Webster's New World Dictionary, College Edition, The World Publishing Company, USA, 1957.

Gothard, Bill, Rebuilder's Guide, Institute in Basic Life Principles, USA, 1982.

Harris, R. Laird, and Gleason L. Archer, and Bruce Waltke, Theological Wordbook of the Old Testament, Moody Press, Chicago, Illinois, 1980.

Kylstra, Chester and Betst, Restoring the Foundations, Proclaiming His Word, Inc., Pensacola, Florida, 1994.

Lucado, Max, When God Whispers Your Name, Word Publishing, 1994

McManus, Michael J., Marriage Savers, Zondervan Publishing House, Grand Rapids, Michigan, 1993, 1995.

Morford, William J., The Power New Testament: Revealing Jewish Roots (translation of the 1993 Fourth Edition United Bible Society Greek Manuscript) William J. Morford, Lakeland, Florida, 1996.

Penner, Clifford and Joyce, The Gift of Sex, A Christian Guide to Sexual Fulfillment, Word Books, Waco, Texas, 1981.

Roeder, Linda L., upRIGHTing RELATIONSHIPS, Parson's Publishing House, Stafford, Virginia, 2013.

Smalley, Gary, (with Steve Scott), If Only He Knew, Zondervan Publishing House, Grand Rapids, Michigan, 1982.

Stoop, David, Experiencing God Together, Tyndale House Publisher, Inc. Wheaton, Illinois, 1982.

Strong, James, The New Strong's Exhaustive Concordance of the Bible, Thomas Nelson, Inc., Nashville, Tennessee, 1984.

Vine, William E., and Merrill F. Unger, and William White, Jr., Vine's Complete Expository Dictionary of the Old and New Testament Words, Thomas Nelson, Inc., Nashville, Tennessee, 1985.

Weaver II, Richard L., Understanding Interpersonal Communication, 7th Edition, Harper Collins, New York, 1996.

Wheat, M.D., Ed and Wheat, Gaye. Intended for Pleasure, Fleming H. Revell, Grand Rapids, Michigan, 1997.

Wilson, Sandra D., Hurt People Hurt People, Thomas Nelson Publishers, Nashville, Tennessee, 1993.

TABLE OF CONTENTS

SESSION ONE 1
Waiver (Optional: for those receiving ministry) 3
Before You Begin, Phases, Introduction 5
Questionnaires: Engaged Couple, Married Couple 9
Study Guide #1a: God's Design, Order, and Purpose for Marriage .. 13
Study Guide #1b: Repentance and Forgiveness........................ 18-20
INDIVIDUAL ASSIGNMENT #1 and questions to answer...... 5,6,7,9 or 11,21
FIRST JOINT SESSION.. 23-24

SESSION TWO 25
Study Guide #2a: Prayer 27
Study Guide #2b: Johari Window 35
Study Guide #2c: Identifying and Sharing Feelings 43
INDIVIDUAL ASSIGNMENT #2 and questions to answer............. 33,44,46,48
SECOND JOINT SESSION... 51-52

SESSION THREE 53
Study Guide #3a: Resolving Feelings 55
Study Guide #3b Listening Skills: Feedback 61
Study Guide #3c Healthy Communication Pattern 63
Study Guide #3d Giving and Receiving Input............................. 65-66
INDIVIDUAL ASSIGNMENT #3 and questions to answer............. 59,62,64,67
THIRD JOINT SESSION 69

SESSION FOUR 71
Study Guide #4a: Codependency 73
Study Guide #4b: Disagreements and Differences 77
Study Guide #4c: Amends.. 80
Study Guide #4d: Restoration 81
INDIVIDUAL ASSIGNMENT #4 .... 74, 79, 81
FOURTH JOINT SESSION 83

SESSION FIVE 85
Study Guide #5a: Husband and Wife 87
Study Guide #5b: Submission and Unity 95
Study Guide #5c: Breaking Habits (Optional) 99
   INDIVIDUAL ASSIGNMENTS #5a,b,c & questions to answer..89,91-94,98,101,104
FIFTH JOINT SESSION 107

SESSION SIX 109
Study Guide #6a: Vision and Five Year Plan 113
Study Guide #6b: Budget 115
Study Guide #6c: Sexuality 127
INDIVIDUAL ASSIGNMENT #6 and questions to answer: Masters (Below) Plus 132
MASTERS FOR FORMS 113-114,117,119,121
SIXTH JOINT SESSION 135-137

SESSION ONE, pp. 3-21

SESSION ONE

Waiver (Optional: only for those receiving ministry.)	3
Before You Begin	5
Phases	6
Introduction	7
Questionnaire Engaged Couple	9
Questionnaire: Married Couple	11
Study Guide #1a.: God's Design, Order, and Purpose for Marriage	13
Study Guide #1b: Repentance and Forgiveness	19
INDIVIDUAL ASSIGNMENT #1 and questions to answer	5,6,7,9 or 11,21
FIRST JOINT SESSION	23

IF YOU ARE COMPLETING THIS AS A SELF HELP WORKBOOK:

1. Each person should complete all reading and answer all questions on pages 5-21. **Always highlight or underline** significant points as you read assignments. Please fill in every blank and answer all questions, as you will need these answers for your joint sessions.
2. On the date you set for your joint session (see schedule on page 7), meet with your spouse/fiancée to complete together the Joint Session #1 on pages 23-24.

IF YOU ARE RECEIVING MINISTRY:

1. Complete the Waiver of Liability and Confidentiality on page 3.
2. Complete all reading and answer all questions on pages 5-21. **Always highlight or underline** significant points as you read assignments. Please fill in every blank and answer all questions, as you will need these answers for your ministry session.
3. Turn in your Waiver and your completed Questionnaires to your ministry team 1-2 weeks prior to ministry, as requested.
4. When assigned, meet with your spouse/fiancée to complete together the Joint Session #1 on pages 23-24.

The Intimate Marriage (5)
© 2013 Paraklesis Ministries

SESSION ONE, pp. 3-21

SESSION ONE, pp. 3-21

WAIVER OF LIABILITY AND CONFIDENTIALITY

Name (Spouse or Fiancée #1)		
Address		
City Zip		Zip
Phone	Home	Cell

Name (Spouse or Fiancée #2)		
Address		
City Zip		Zip
Phone	Home	Cell

Waiver of Liability

I am aware that this ministry process may need to be supplemented with other lay ministry, or professional care for specialized treatment. I will seek additional care if needs arise that cannot be resolved during this ministry.

I accept the fact that Christian International Central/CI Family Worship Center, my ministry leader(s) and Paraklesis Ministries will provide Christian Biblical ministry, not professional or psychological counseling. I fully understand and agree that the outcome of my ministry is solely in the hands of the Holy Spirit (God), and that therefore, the church or any personal minister cannot be considered responsible for any results, consequences, or effects, or lack thereof, which I may experience as a result of this ministry. I am not aware of any issues which could make this an inappropriate level of ministry in my situation. I am responsible for obtaining any necessary follow-up counseling to deal with any issues which are not resolved through this process. I hold my ministry leader(s), Christian International, Christian International Central, Christian International Family Worship Center and Paraklesis Ministries harmless and not liable for the outcome of this ministry. **I waive all rights for claims of liability.**

I am aware that I may request referral for professional counseling or for other ministry which I may desire. I am aware that the names of several local counseling services are available to me upon my request.

Waiver of Confidentiality

I am aware that all statements I make to my ministry leader(s) may be of a confidential nature, including all written information, and that my ministry leader will not disclose them without my consent, except as may be required by law. **However, I waive my right to confidentiality at the discretion of my ministry leader(s), particularly in the following situations:**

1. My ministry leader(s) may give a summary report of the results of the ministry to the oversight person I have named below.
2. My ministry leader(s) may consult with the oversight ministry team, the appropriate leadership, and/or their designated representatives concerning their ministry to me.
3. I acknowledge that pastors, counselors, ministry leader(s) or any other persons involved in working with adults or children in a helping setting are either encouraged or required by law to disclose to the appropriate person, agency, or civil authority any harm or potential harm that a person may attempt or desire to do to himself or others.
4. I acknowledge that pastors, counselors, ministry leader(s) or any other persons involved in working with adults or children in a helping setting are either encouraged or required by law to report any reasonable suspicion of physical or sexual abuse that has been done or is being done to a minor child.
5. As otherwise required by law or when my ministry leader in their sole discretion thinks that it is in my best interest, or the best interests of others, for them to disclose.

Please send the summary report of my ministry to the person who provides my oversight., named below:

Receiver#1		Phone	
Address			
City		'State	Zip

Receiver#2		Phone	
Address			
City		'State	Zip

By my signature below I acknowledge that I have read and understand all of the above provisions, including the Waiver of Liability and Waiver of Confidentiality, and that I accept the stated conditions and limits of liability and confidentiality.

Signature #1	Signature #2
Printed Name	Printed Name
Date	Date

The Intimate Marriage (5)
© 2013 Paraklesis Ministries

SESSION ONE, pp. 3-21

SESSION ONE, pp. 3-21

BEFORE YOU BEGIN …

📖 **"Being confident of this very thing, that He which hath begun a good work in you will perform it until the day of Jesus Christ."** (Ph1:6)

God completes every good work He begins. According to this verse, He's going to take our whole lifetime to complete what He has begun in us

The fact that you are interested in this ministry process indicates that you desire to grow and to allow the Lord to change you so that your marriage will reach its fullest potential. But even the most ambitious Christian may resist change. If we have allowed the Lord to deal with us in a certain area and we are enjoying the fruits of His work, we may think we have a right to "camp out" at that level. We may consider it strength. Although the Lord may be pleased with what He has accomplished in us, He won't be satisfied until He has completed what He has begun. So resist the urge to resist change! Let the Lord do all He desires in you.

📖 **"But I will reprove thee, and set them in order in thine eyes."** (Ps.50:21b)

Because of His wisdom and mercy, the Holy Spirit doesn't convict us of all of our sins at once. Step by step, He reveals to us the areas in which He is at work. In an orderly way, He convicts us first of one fault and then another. As we repent and allow Him to change us, He matures us and develops our character.

📖 **"Iron sharpeneth iron …"** (Pr. 27:17)

Just as the Lord has a plan for the work He is doing in you, He has a plan and an order for the work He is doing in your partner. Did you ever stop to think that the areas in your partner's life that He leaves temporarily untouched are for the purpose of maturing you?

Let us encourage you to allow the Holy Spirit to change you. Avoid the temptation to pressure your partner to change. The Holy Spirit knows just what is needed.

1. Do you focus more on the changes your partner needs to make or on the changes you need to make? _____

2. Would your partner agree with your answer? _____

SESSION ONE, pp. 3-21

PHASES: LIFE AND RELATIONSHIP SKILL MINISTRY

Ideally, as people activate these skills in their lives and relationships, they go through a series of progressive changes (Phases), each building upon the previous level.

<u>PHASE ONE</u>: The focus is on identifying your personal issues and learning to apply the relationship skills.
- Avoid co-dependency.
    - Focus on the personal changes you need to make.
    - Give others the space and time they need to work through their own issues.

<u>PHASE TWO</u>: Continue to practice skills and to work on your personal issues. Begin to focus on your relationship with your spouse or fiancée.

<u>PHASE THREE</u>: Continue to practice skills and to work on your personal issues. Continue to give priority to your relationship with your spouse or fiancée. On Phase Three, you will add a focus on your relationships with immediate family members.
- Focus on improving relationships within your immediate family.
    - Forgive each one, as needed.
    - Repent to each one, as needed.
    - If married, resolve any in-law issues by prioritizing the marriage relationship and communicating the changes to the in laws if necessary.
- For parents: As a mother-father team or as a single parent:
    - Develop written house rules and consequences.
    - Use the Brainstorming technique at some point in this process to include input from your spouse or fiancée (if you are engaged or married) and then at an appropriate age, to incorporate consideration of the children's input.
- If you are a parent, teach your children new skills that are appropriate for their age: communication, resolution, praying together, budgeting, vision, and sexuality. Also add their insights and discernment to the family vision.

<u>PHASE FOUR</u>: Continue to work on personal issues and to apply these skills to your marriage and immediate family relationships. Begin to focus also on relationships at work or school, extended family, friends, and other outside relationships
- Strengthen relationships with peers and authority figures at work and/or at church.
- Special attention should be given to resolving workplace relationships and relationships with authority figures that have been unhealthy or unsuccessful.

<u>PHASE FIVE</u>: Continue to work on personal issues and to apply skills to your family relationships and to outside relationships. Begin to focus on reaching out to help and to teach others, using the new skills you have gained.

1. What phase are you on now?	2. What is your focus?

SESSION ONE, pp. 3-21

INTRODUCTION

This material is based upon a biblical view of marriage. Your workbook will become a permanent record of this very important time in your lives and a reference upon which you can build and expand the vision for your marriage.

If you are completing this workbook with the help of a minister or a counselor, please record your ministry session dates on the chart below. **Prior to each ministry session**, read the assigned Study Guide(s), filling in every blank and answering all questions on your Individual Assignment. The effectiveness of your sessions will hinge upon your faithful completion of all required reading and written assignments, which are the basis for your next session. Please contact your ministers if you have questions so that you can come to each session fully prepared. You will complete the related Joint Session with your partner after the completion of all of your ministry sessions.

If you are completing this workbook with your fiancée or spouse, without the assistance of a minister or counselor: Each of you should read a Study Guide, fill in any blanks, and answer all of the questions prior to meeting with each other to complete the related Joint Session. Please schedule six dates on which you and your partner will meet to complete your Joint Sessions. Record these dates on the chart below. If you complete one Study Guide and meet for one Joint Session that same week, it will take you six weeks to complete the workbook.

As you diligently seek the Lord about your relationship, we ask Him to reveal His great love for you and to impart to you His abundant grace for your relationship.

BEFORE YOUR FIRST SESSION, each person should:

☐ Read pp. 5-20, Complete the Individual Assignment on p. 21.	☐ Complete questionnaire on pp. 9-10 (engaged couples) or 11-12 (married couples).
☐ If you are receiving ministry, complete the waiver on p. 3 and give the waiver and your completed questionnaires to your ministry team two weeks prior to your first session.	

SCHEDULE: Record below your ministry session dates. Or, if you are doing this as a self help workbook, record your joint session dates here. If you miss a session, record a make up date.

SESSION #	TIMES (from____ to ___)	DAY/DATE
1st		
2nd		
3rd		
4th		
5th		
6th		
Make up session		
Make up session		

SESSION ONE, pp. 3-21

SESSION ONE, pp. 3-21

ENGAGED COUPLE QUESTIONNAIRE

Name _____ Date _____

Please complete this questionnaire and your waiver and return to your ministry team 1-2 weeks prior to your first session. Use separate paper to continue answers as needed.

1. WEDDING INFORMATION

    Date _____ Time _____ Location _____

    Who will perform the ceremony? _____

    Have you confirmed your plans with this person? _____

2. Are you saved? _____ If "yes", when and how did you receive the Lord? _____

3. Are you a member of a church? _____ The name of your church _____

4. Are you baptized in the Holy Spirit? _____ Do you speak in tongues? _____

5. Briefly describe your past and present relationship with each parent (natural and step)

    Natural father _____

    Natural mother _____

    Step father _____

    Step mother _____

6. Status of parent's marriage? _____

7. Describe several strengths in your relationship with your fiancée. _____

8. What marriage problems are you especially concerned about preventing? _____

9. Do have any children? _____ Do you have custody? _____ Have you been married before? _____ Please give details _____

10. Have you ever experienced physical, emotional, verbal or sexual abuse? _____ Has this ever occurred in your relationship with your fiancé? _____

    (If yes, please explain) _____

11. Have you ever used or abused drugs or any chemicals? ___ Have you ever thought that you or your partner might have a problem with alcohol? _____ (You) _____ (Partner). If you answered "yes", please see "Breaking Habits" on pages 100-106.

SESSION ONE, pp. 3-21

12. If you answered yes to either question #10 and/or 11, we strongly encourage you to seek ministry or counseling if you have not previously or if the issues are not fully resolved. Please list options you have selected or are considering: _____
_____
_____

13. Have you ever received Restoring the Foundations Ministry? ____ (Year____) If yes, please list Godly and Ungodly beliefs and the main areas of ministry you received on separate paper. Share these with your fiancée and talk about how they could impact your marriage.

Some Suggestions:

It is often advisable to have a physical exam prior to marriage. If desired, birth control decisions can be discussed at this time. (Some require weeks or months of preparation prior to marriage)

Having a written budget for the wedding and honeymoon will eliminate unnecessary stress and is strongly recommended. See suggested format, below:

PERSON RESPONSIBLE	ITEM	ESTIMATED COST

GOD BLESS YOU!

SESSION ONE, pp. 3-21

MARRIED COUPLE QUESTIONNAIRE

Please complete this questionnaire and your waiver and return to your ministry team on the date requested, usually 1-2 weeks prior to your first session. Use separate paper to continue answers as needed.

1. Name of spouse _____

2. Spouse's occupation _____ Hours worked per week _____ Your occupation _____ Hours worked per week _____

3. How long did you know each other before your marriage? _____

4. Ages at time of marriage: You _____ and Your spouse _____

5. Length of current marriage _____

6. Number of children _____

7. How many children still at home? _____ Their ages _____

8. Any previous marriages? _____ Details: _____
   _____
   _____

9. Are you saved? _____ If "yes", when and how did you receive the Lord? _____
   _____

10. Are you baptized in the Holy Spirit? _____. Do you speak in tongues? _____

11. Your Church _____
    Pastor's name _____

12. Do you attend regularly? _____

13. Describe your relationship with the Lord _____
    _____

The Intimate Marriage (5)
© 2013 Paraklesis Ministries

SESSION ONE, pp. 3-21

14. Describe your relationship with your spouse _____

15. What relationship skills would you like to strengthen? _____

16. Have you ever experienced physical, emotional, verbal, or sexual abuse? _____ Has this ever occurred in your relationship with your spouse? (Details) _____

17. Have you ever used or abused drugs or any chemicals? _____ Have you ever thought that you might have a problem with alcohol? _____ Your Partner? _____ If you answered "yes" for either of you, please see "Breaking Habits" on page 99-105.

18. If you answered yes to either questions #16 and/or 17, we strongly encourage you to seek ministry or counseling if you have not previously or if the issues are not fully resolved. Please list options you selected or will consider: _____

19. Have you ever received Restoring The Foundations Ministry? _____ Year? _____ If yes, please list your Godly and Ungodly Beliefs and the main areas of ministry you received on separate paper. Share these with your spouse and discuss the ways they may be affecting your marriage. _____

GOD BLESS YOU!

SESSION ONE, pp. 3-21

STUDY GUIDE #1a
GOD'S DESIGN, PURPOSE, AND ORDER FOR MARRIAGE
Read and highlight or underline

1. MARRIAGE: GOD'S DESIGN

When we make a garment or build a piece of furniture, we generally begin with a pattern. We begin with a picture of the finished product in mind, and then we proceed according to the plans, carefully constructing each piece to match the original pattern. With this method, our finished product closely resembles the picture we observed before we began the project.

In this session, you will study God's design, purpose and order for marriage so that your view of marriage lines up with God's pattern for marriage. These basic Scriptural truths can be applied to establish a new marriage on a firm foundation, to strengthen a good marriage, or to restore a painful or dysfunctional relationship. God's Word works! Many couples, so in love at the time of their wedding, have veered off course because they never had this godly foundation in place. The fruitfulness of a marriage relationship is evidence of the strength and the quality of the foundation that has been laid. It is never too late to strengthen or straighten the foundation of a relationship.

> 📖 **"For other foundation can no man lay than that is laid, which is Jesus Christ."** (1Co.3:11)
> Jesus Christ is the substance, the essential element, of your marriage.

> 📖 **"And if one prevail against him, two shall withstand him; and a threefold cord is not quickly broken."** (Ec.4:12)

HUSBAND + JESUS + WIFE

> 📖 **"Male and female created he them; and blessed them, and called their name Adam in the day when they were created."** (Ge.5:2)

God called **them** Adam.

At the time of creation, Eve was **in** Adam.

They were literally ONE FLESH!

> 📖 **"And the Lord caused a deep sleep to fall on Adam, and he slept, and he took one of his ribs, and closed up the flesh instead thereof. And the rib, which the Lord had taken from man, made he a woman, and brought her unto the man. And Adam said, This is now bone of my bones, flesh of my flesh: she shall be called Woman because she was taken out of Man. Therefore shall a man leave his father and mother, and shall cleave unto his wife: and they shall be one flesh."** (Ge.2:21-24)

Prophetically, Adam declared that he and Eve were one flesh. He began their relationship with this revelation in mind. At the time of a marriage, there is a spiritual joining of two to become one flesh. There is a physical union, but the manifestation of that unity in the relationship is a process that continues throughout the entire marriage.

The Intimate Marriage (5)
© 2013 Paraklesis Ministries

SESSION ONE, pp. 3-21

1 X 1 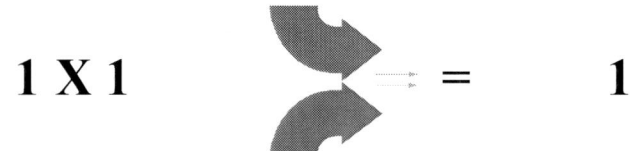 = 1

According to the Theological Wordbook of the Old Testament[1], the word "one" in this passage "stresses unity while recognizing diversity within that oneness". When a man and woman marry, they become one flesh. By the strength of the covenant, a new relationship exists, one that did not exist before. This relationship does not eliminate each partner's individual purpose, interests and gifting, but rather, it blends them and multiplies their effectiveness. The more a husband and wife mature spiritually, the more they reflect a unique facet of the beauty of God.

📖 **"Wherefore they are no more twain, but one flesh. What therefore God hath joined together, let not man put asunder." (Mt.19:6)**
When God fashioned Eve out of Adam's rib, she became Adam's companion, but God still viewed them as ONE and related to them as ONE. Marriage is a covenant relationship, ordained by God to last a lifetime.

📖 **"It is not good that the man should be alone; I will make an help meet for him." (Ge.2:18)**
In his Marriage Course, John Fichtner gives an excellent exposition of this passage. He states that the title "help meet" (Neged in Hebrew) refers to "a helper suitable for completing him."[2]

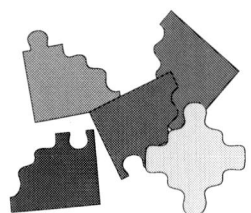 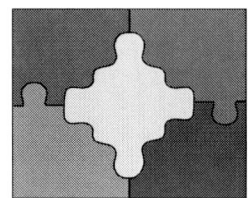

2. MARRIAGE: GOD'S PURPOSE

> GOD WANTS YOU TO BE A
> REFLECTION OF CHRIST AND HIS
> LOVE FOR THE CHURCH

📖 **"For this cause shall a man leave his father and mother, and shall be joined unto his wife, and they two shall be one flesh. This is a great mystery: but I speak concerning Christ and the church. Nevertheless, let everyone of you inparticular so love his wife even as himself; and the wife see that she reverence her husband." (Ep.5:31-33)**

---

[1] Harris, Archer and Waltke, Theological Wordbook of the Old Testament, vol.1. (Chicago, Illinois: The Moody Bible Institute, 1980) 30.
[2] John Fichtner, Marriage Course, (Marietta, Georgia: Liberty Church 1991) 4.

SESSION ONE, pp. 3-21

📖 "Fulfill ye my joy that ye be like-minded, having the same love, being of one accord, of one mind. Let nothing be done through strife or vainglory; but in lowliness of mind let each esteem other better than themselves. Look not every man on his own things, but every man also on the things of others. Let this mind be in you, which was also in Christ Jesus: Who, being in the form of God, thought it not robbery to be equal with God: but made himself of no reputation, and took upon him the form of a servant, and was made in the likeness of men: And being found in fashion as a man, he humbled himself, and became obedient unto death, even the death of the cross." (Ph.2:2-8)

Jesus is the "second Adam". His bride, the church, was birthed out of his pierced side. From the manger to the cross, the pattern that He set when He loved the church is that He gave up every right and laid down His life for us.

GOD WANTS TO CHANGE YOU!

📖 "So God created man in His own image, in the image of God created he him; male and female created he them." (Ge.1:27)

📖 "Iron sharpeneth iron; so a man sharpeneth the countenance of his friend." (Pr.27:17)

The marriage relationship is not often a "smooth fit" from the beginning. There are differences of opinion and even character flaws which may cause friction and pressure. Although human nature often resists change, maturity will require change. This is just as God intended it to be! He is molding us into His image, and He uses our partners as a part of this process. He knows what we need in a mate.

📖 "Husbands, love your wives, even as Christ loved the church, and gave himself for it; that he might sanctify and cleanse it with the washing of the water by the word, that he might present it to himself a glorious church, not having spot or wrinkle, or any such thing; but that it should be holy and without blemish. No man ever yet hated his own flesh; but nourisheth and cherisheth it, even as the Lord the church." (Ep.5:25-29)

In a marriage relationship, God provides opportunities for sanctification, healing, edification and restoration. As husbands and/or wives walk in intimacy with God, listening to and heeding His logos and rhema word, they are transformed, over time, into His likeness.

GOD HAS A PURPOSE FOR YOUR MARRIAGE !

📖 "And God blessed them, and God said unto them, Be fruitful and multiply, and replenish the earth, and subdue it ..." (Ge.1:28)

Although children are the "fruit of the womb", this Scripture says to be fruitful AND to multiply. To be fruitful is to be productive, to fulfill your purpose.

The Intimate Marriage (5)
© 2013 Paraklesis Ministries

SESSION ONE, pp. 3-21

📖 **"For we are laborers together with God: ye are God's husbandry, ye are God's building." (1Co.3:9)**
Although God desires that you would have an excellent marriage, His intention goes far beyond providing an ideal environment for you and your family.

3. MARRIAGE: GOD'S ORDER

It is important for newly married couples to simplify their priorities during the first year of marriage so that they can focus upon their relationship with God and with one another. However, it is also true that couples who have never dealt with this issue may need to spend a season re-ordering their priorities.

📖 **"For this cause shall a man leave his father and his mother and cleave unto his wife." (Mk.10:7)**
In order for a couple to "cleave" to one another, they must truly "leave" (i.e. dramatically change their relationship with) their parents. Some of the areas which may be affected by your ability to "leave and cleave" are:
- planning holiday traditions
- making decisions
- choosing a home (location, etc.)
- budgeting (decisions, borrowing, etc.)
- sharing intimate thoughts, feelings and information
  (in general: share with spouse first and most frequently)
- keeping confidences your spouse shares with you
- "covering" one another: Be compassionate about your partner's feelings. Be discrete when wisdom indicates, even if confidentiality has not been requested. Don't tease disrespectfully or reveal sensitive information in front of others.
- speaking highly of one another

SESSION ONE, pp. 3-21

One of the more common problems found in marriage relationships is that of a lack of order. Here are a few examples of problems that can arise in this area:

Lack of order in a marriage is often seen as a lack of attention and time given to the marriage relationship and/or an inordinate amount of time and attention given to subordinate activities such as ministry, job, friendships, television, computer, sports, etc. One of the underlying causes of this problem is a lack of relationship skills. If a spouse feels more competent while involved in their job, ministry, friendships, hobbies or volunteer work, they may place a higher priority upon these activities than they do on the less comfortable priority of relating intimately to their spouse.

People who have a deep-seated belief that their value is based upon the things they accomplish may also unintentionally give lower priority to an intimate relationship with their spouse.

Troubled marriages require special attention. These couples may need to simplify their schedules by the elimination of all unnecessary activities, spending quality time together and/or seeking counsel, until the problems have been resolved.

If a spouse has never truly experienced the process of "leaving and cleaving", he or she may not realize that they are giving precedence to their desire to please their parents over their desire to serve their spouse. In this case, their spouse's discernment, preferences, and opinions are placed on a lower priority than they should be. They may oblige the parents in order to win their approval or to avoid conflict with them, and this can become a higher priority than their relationship with their spouse, or even than their desire to please the Lord. This condition can lead to serious conflict in a marriage.

📖 **"Submitting yourselves one to another in the fear[3] of God. Wives, submit yourselves unto your own husbands as unto the Lord. For the husband is the head of the wife, even as Christ is the head of the church …" (Ep.5:22-23)**
Out of reverence for God, mindful of His desires, a husband and wife relate humbly to one another. God has placed the husband as the head, the leader, and a covering for his wife.

📖 **"But I would have you know, that the head of every man is Christ; and the head of the woman is the man; and the head of Christ is God." (1Co.11:3)**
A wife who is submitted to her husband is really submitted to and trusting in the Lord. A wife who is not submitted to her husband has also removed herself from the protective covering of God.[4] A wife is not to sin in order to submit to her husband, but she can respect, honor, and submit to him in other areas. In fact, she may win him over to the Lord in this way."

GOD
⇩
HUSBAND
⇩
WIFE
⇩
Family ⇄ Job ⇄ Ministry

---

[3] Vine, Unger, White, <u>Vines Expository Dictionary of Old and New Testament Words</u>, (Nashville, Camden New York: Thomas Nelson Publishers, 1984) 229.
[4] Bill Gothard, <u>Rebuilder's Guide,</u> (United States of America: Institute in Basic Life Principles, 1982) 113

SESSION ONE, pp. 3-21

Pastor Henry Wright of Freedom Christian Center in Knoxville, Tennessee says it this way: "Submission brings responsibility." As a wife submits to her husband, God places her under his covering. He feels responsible for her well-being. This is not a relationship marked by control and limitation, but one of mutual respect that provides an atmosphere for the development of the fullest potential of each partner.

📖 **"For I also am a man set under authority, having under me soldiers, and I say unto one, Go, and he goeth; and to another, Come, and he cometh; and to my servant, Do this, and he doeth it." (Lu.7:8)**
A man under authority has authority. A man who is yielded to God has authority. It is likely that a man who has a heart to please God will have a wife who trusts and is at peace. A wife's greatest need is that her husband seek after God.

📖 **"As for my people, children are their oppressors, and women rule over them. O my people, they which lead thee cause thee to err, and destroy the way of thy paths." (Is.3:12)**
This is not to say that the wife is not responsible for her decisions, but it does say that God will hold a husband accountable for a wife who is not submitted if he has caused her to err.

PLEASE CONTINUE WITH SESSION ONE by reading and highlighting or underlining the following study guide ....

STUDY GUIDE #1b
REPENTANCE AND FORGIVENESS

SCRIPTURE STUDY
"God resisteth the proud, but giveth grace unto the humble." (Ja.4:6)

Every couple needs to develop a practice of regularly repenting to one another as the need arises. There are times when we need to repent to our spouse (or fiancée) as well as to God. If this is the case, nothing else will do. Being extra nice and trying to "make it up" won't do. Acting like nothing happened won't do. Only repentance will do! When we avoid repentance, we lack the grace we need for change and we usually continue in the same sin. We receive grace for change when we humbly repent and receive God's forgiveness.

THE ELEMENTS OF REPENTANCE ARE:
1. Genuine sorrow (Psalm 51:17)
2. Confession to God (Luke 15:18)
3. Confession to man, unless it would cause unnecessary pain or harm (Ja.5:16)
4. Change

A repentant heart opens the door to God's grace and therefore, to the ability to change our behavior, thoughts and attitudes. (Ja.4:6)

The Intimate Marriage (5)
© 2013 Paraklesis Ministries

SESSION ONE, pp. 3-21

INHIBITORS OF REPENTANCE:

Condemnation, which leads to defensiveness rather than receptivity to the Holy Spirit and others (Ro.8:1)

1. Pride, wanting to be "right" (Ja.4:6)
2. Tendency to blame others. We're responsible for our own actions, regardless of what others may have done. (Mt.7:5)
3. Tendency to compare
4. Blindness to our own faults (Psa.139:23-24) (Je.17:9)
5. Tendency to resist change
6. Fear of God's anger

HELPERS OF REPENTANCE:

1. Prompt obedience to the Holy Spirit when He shows us that repentance is necessary. (1Ti.4:2)
2. Humility (Ja.4:8-10)
3. Teachable attitude (Co.1:28)
4. Rehearse the past … where did this behavior lead in the past?
5. Compassion toward the one we have offended. "And be ye kind to one another, tenderhearted, forgiving one another, even as God for Christ's sake hath forgiven you." (Eph.4:32)

REMEMBER:

1. When someone comes to us about information that is in our "blind spot", it may not seem to apply! The Holy Spirit can open our eyes if we are receptive and humble. Even when we are not "wrong", it is possible that our style or methods may cause others undue discomfort. If we are compassionate and repentant rather than defensive, it will strengthen our relationship.

2. Our "enemies" often speak to us about issues others may avoid. Instead of automatically discounting things that they say, if we will open our hearts to the Holy Spirit, He may use what they share to help us to see an area of need in ourselves.

3. Sin may be a behavior, but it may also be an attitude or a thought we entertain. God is very interested in what is in our hearts, and He wants to cleanse us of the beliefs and attitudes that are not pleasing to Him. It is the grace that comes with repentance and forgiveness that will enable us to be changed.

HOW TO REPENT:

1. Receive the conviction of the Holy Spirit.
2. Forgive others, as necessary.
3. Confess to the person and ask their forgiveness (Unless it would cause unnecessary pain. Don't make excuses or minimize what you have done.
4. Listen compassionately to their feedback.
5. Confess to God.

SESSION ONE, pp. 3-21

6. Take a moment to receive God's forgiveness.
7. Ask the Holy Spirit to show you the change you need to make.
8. Share this change with the other person.
9. Forgive yourself.
10. Do all of this with a pure heart. Even if it takes a while for the feelings to catch up, you can repent, knowing that God will complete the work He has begun in you.
11. This process takes practice. Study and apply the points above on a regular basis, until they have become "second nature" to you.

WHAT ABOUT FORGIVENESS?

1. "We must forgive as soon as we are aware of the need, even if the person never asks for our forgiveness or repents to us. (Mt.18:33-35). Unforgiveness only hurts the one who holds it.
2. Jesus set the pattern for forgiveness with His first words on the cross : "Father, forgive them" (Lu.23:34)
3. Jesus forgave us while we were still sinners (Ro.5:8), how could we do any less?
4. 1Peter 4:8 (AMP) and Eph.2:14&21 (NIV)
5. Forgiveness does not mean that what happened was all right, it means that we agree to release the situation and let the Lord deal with it!
6. See page 58 for healing of hurts, which is often a part of the complete forgiveness process. If any hurt remains in a memory, it is likely that there is still some unforgiveness. It may be a process that requires additional forgiveness and healing over time.

 Compete your Individual assignment on page 21 now.

SESSION ONE, pp. 3-21

INDIVIDUAL ASSIGNMENT #1
(Continue answers on separate paper if necessary)

1. How firmly do you think your relationship is founded upon Jesus Christ? _____

2. Please describe one way in which you have had to change/grow because of your marriage or courtship _____
_____

3. List one quality you appreciated in your fiancée / spouse when you first met them. _____
_____

   List two reasons that you are glad that the Lord brought you together. _____
   _____
   _____

   List one quality that you respect or admire in your fiancée/spouse _____
   _____

   On a separate piece of paper, write a brief love letter to your partner (3-4 sentences), based on the information you just listed. Take this letter to your first Joint Session.

4. As you read the section on "God's Order for Marriage" on pages 16-18, what needs did you identify in your own marriage? _____
_____
_____

5. How easy is it for you to go to your partner to repent when you are wrong? (Are you in the habit of repenting to people as necessary?) _____
_____

6. When was the last time you asked your partner to forgive you? _____

7. Would you be willing to show compassion by asking your partner's forgiveness, even if you believe you weren't wrong? _____

8. Please list anything for which you sense the Holy Spirit is asking you to ask your partner's forgiveness. _____
_____

The Intimate Marriage (5)
© 2013 Paraklesis Ministries

SESSION ONE, pp. 3-21

FIRST JOINT SESSION, pp.23-24

FIRST JOINT SESSION

Chose a location in which you can be alone and in which you both feel comfortable sharing intimately with one another. Take a few moments together to prepare the room if necessary. Some couples enjoy soft music, candles, and refreshments. Make the atmosphere pleasant and conducive to a special time together during each of your joint sessions.

OPEN IN PRAYER

Invite the Holy Spirit. Pray as He leads. Each person should express the desires of your heart for this time.

#1. FOR ENGAGED COUPLES ONLY:

Read and discuss the Love and Purity teaching, page 133. Pray together as the Holy Spirit leads, repenting to each other and to the Lord if necessary. Ask Him to strengthen you and thank Him for His grace.

What steps are you currently taking to assure purity in your physical relationship? _____

_____

_____

#1. FOR MARRIED COUPLES ONLY:

Read "Love and Purity", on page 133.

If you did not adhere to a godly standard in the area of physical intimacy before marriage, especially if you had a mutual agreement to remain pure, there may be an unwillingness to submit and trust now, even if it is many years later. If one person was the initiator, the other one may blame them and still hold this against them, but both need to ask God's forgiveness if they have participated.

Take turns sharing with each other: Do you think it is possible that any of the difficulties you experience in the area of submission date back to a lack of trust which may have stemmed from your physical relationship while you were dating? _____

- Do you need to repent and/or forgive because of sexual experiences during your dating relationship? _____

FIRST JOINT SESSION, pp.23-24

- Ask the Lord to lead you as you pray together now, repenting and forgiving as necessary.

- Take a few moments to listen to the Lord, then journal any words of ministry or direction that He reveals to you:

#2. FOR ALL COUPLES:
- Discuss the points that you have underlined on pages 18-20 (Repentance and Forgiveness).
- Repent to the Lord and to one another, referring to your list on #8 on page 21. Forgive one another, forgive yourself, ask the Lord to give you a heart that is increasingly humble.

#3. EXCHANGE THE LETTERS YOU WROTE TO EACH OTHER (see #3, p. 21).

#4. CLOSE BY PRAYING OVER EACH OTHER.
    Confirm the time for your next joint session.

SESSION TWO, pp. 27-49

SESSION TWO
Study Guide #2a: Prayer 27
Study Guide #2b: Johari Window 34
Study Guide #2c: Identifying and Sharing Feelings 41
INDIVIDUAL ASSIGNMENTS #2a,b,c and questions to answer 33,44,46,48
SECOND JOINT SESSION.. 51-52

IF YOU ARE COMPLETING THIS AS A SELF HELP WORKBOOK:
1. Each person should complete all reading and answer all questions on pages 27-49. **Highlight or underline** significant points as you read. Please fill in every blank and answer all questions, as you will need these answers for your joint sessions.
2. On the date you set for your joint session (see schedule on page 7), meet with your spouse/fiancée to complete together the Joint Session #2 on pages 51-52.

IF YOU ARE RECEIVING MINISTRY:
a) Complete all reading and answer all questions on pages 27-49. **Highlight or underline** significant points as you read. Please fill in every blank and answer all questions, as you will need these answers for your ministry session.
b) When assigned, meet with your spouse/fiancée to complete together the Joint Session #2 on pages 51-52.

The Intimate Marriage (5)
© 2013 Paraklesis Ministries

SESSION TWO, pp. 27-49

SESSION TWO, pp. 27-49

STUDY GUIDE #2a
PRAYER: COMMUNICATING WITH GOD

PRAYING TOGETHER

Picture yourself in a canoe on a sunny day. Now imagine that you are paddling upstream, against a rushing current.... and someone else is in the boat paddling in the opposite direction! This is how many people feel as they try to establish the discipline of prayer in their lives. Trying to pray consistently with another person presents even greater difficulty. Our flesh resists the discipline required for a consistent prayer life. The enemy does all he can to keep us from praying, especially from praying with our spouse. Be encouraged, however. God's grace in this area is more than sufficient to allow us to be victorious! He knows the powerful effect of prayer and He also knows the synergistic effects of spending time with someone else in prayer.

Some people have already established the essential discipline of regular personal prayer time in their lives, while others have never successfully instituted this practice. Regardless of their previous experience with individual prayer, incorporating mutual prayer into an engaged or married couples' lives can be challenging. Many people find that their commitment to prayer is weakened by stress or by changes in personal routine, such as getting married or working through problems in a marriage or family. It would seem that difficulties would drive us to pray more than ever, but this is often not the case.

One of the main reasons that we have found that couples avoid mutual prayer is that it requires them to make several decisions every day....just so they can pray together! They must choose the time and the place they'll pray, how long they'll pray, what kinds of prayer they will use, and where they will pray. I think you get the picture. Often, busy couples don't pray together because they don't have a plan. In this lesson, you will learn to develop a plan, a "pattern of prayer", that helps many couples to avoid some of the most common reasons for a lack of mutual prayer time. Most people find that after they follow this structured pattern for a while, they begin to experience more and more freedom in their times of prayer. (The law, structure, leads to freedom. Ge.3:24-25). We recommend that couples have individual prayer times and then also pray together daily. However, we would rather see them spend time in prayer together faithfully two or three times a week than to set a goal to pray together daily, but only accomplish this sporadically.

It is communion with God that gives life and vitality to marriage, but I heard Dutch Sheets say one time that if we pray for any reason other than relationship with the Lord, we will eventually lose interest and stop praying. In his book, Experiencing God Together, David Stoop says "To pray together is not just a simple activity we add to our day. It is an act of aggression against spiritual forces.

📖 **"Jesus said "That if two of you shall agree on earth as touching anything that they shall ask, it shall be done for them of my Father which is in heaven." (Mt.18:19)**
A couple who learns to discern the will of God and to agree with Him in their prayers is effective and powerful!

SESSION TWO, pp. 27-49

THE IMPORTANCE OF LISTENING AS A PART OF PRAYER

Imagine a relationship in which you did all the talking and the other person never commented or gave a response. Now reflect upon these questions:

a. How close would you feel to that person?

b. How well would you know them?

c. How much would you trust them?

d. How often would you want to be with them?

Sometimes, when we don't give the Lord an opportunity to speak into our lives, if we don't take time to listen to what He has to say, we lose the desire to be with Him and to become like Him. We don't even realize that we have unintentionally cut ourselves off from intimacy with Him.

Because the Holy Spirit is THE counselor, it is essential that we be able to hear from Him. People's words may bring comfort or direction at the time they are given, but the words of the Holy Spirit are strength, hope and life to us. A person who has been equipped to hear from God may continue to receive the counsel of the Holy Spirit throughout their life.

> 📖 **"But the friend of the bridegroom, which standeth and heareth him, rejoiceth greatly because of the bridegroom's voice: this my joy therefore is fulfilled." Jn.3:29**

One of the greatest joys in prayer is in hearing the voice of the Lord. Often, when we pray, we think of what we want to say to God, of how we want to intercede, or how we want to thank and praise Him. These are all fundamental aspects of prayer. They are necessary. However, when you think about it, isn't it essential to make opportunity to be quiet and to <u>hear</u> what He has to say to us? Make it a habit to go to Him with questions and listen for His answers. At other times, go to Him without a specific question or agenda and just give Him time to talk and to reveal whatever is on His heart.

> 📖 **"The words that I speak to you, they are spirit and they are life." Jn.6:63b.**

These are rhema words that God speaks to us. They are fresh, presently proceeding from God's heart to ours.

One of the more common causes of dryness in our relationship with God, or a lack of motivation to pray is that we have not made opportunity to hear what God wants to tell us. It is His voice that makes our prayer times come alive.

> 📖 **"O my dove, thou that art in the clefts of the rock, in the secret places of the stairs, let me see thy countenance, let me hear thy voice; for sweet is thy voice, and thy countenance is lovely." Song of Sol.2:14**

28 The Intimate Marriage (5)
© 2013 Paraklesis Ministries

SESSION TWO, pp. 27-49

> 📖 "**And I will give thee the treasures of darkness, and hidden riches of secret places, that thou mayest know that I, the Lord, which call thee by thy name, am the God of Israel.**" Is.45:3

It is in these hidden places that we see the heart of the Lord and fall more and more in love with Him.

HEARING FROM GOD

It is essential to be able to hear from the Holy Spirit as you go through this relationship building process. In this exercise, you will learn how to improve your skill in recognizing God's voice.

Some typical hindrances to hearing from the Lord are:
- Guilt or shame that causes fear of what the Lord would say if we listened. (Habukkuk expected to be reproved, but God gave him a great vision.)
- Not recognizing God's voice
- Not being accustomed to listening for God
- Hurts which have been blamed on the Lord instead of the enemy.[5]
- Confusion or hopelessness about the situation.
- Fear about what the Lord would require of us if He spoke.
- Painful relationships with authority figures (parents, pastors, etc.)

Ask the Holy Spirit to show you any hindrances to your ability to hear His voice, and list them here:

_____
_____
_____
_____
_____
_____
_____

PRAY
1. Break your agreement with any decisions you have made. (e.g. "I am afraid to listen because …" "I can't hear God.")
2. Repent.
3. Forgive, as necessary.
4. Express your desire for more intimacy with the Lord and ask Him to open your ears to hear what His Spirit is saying.

---

[5] **Betsy and Chester Kylstra, Restoring the Foundations (Santa Rosa Beach, Florida: Proclaiming His Word, Inc. 1994) 120-122.**

SESSION TWO, pp. 27-49

RECOGNIZING GOD'S VOICE
> "And when he putteth forth his own sheep, he goeth before them, and the sheep follow him: for they know his voice." Jn.10:4

It takes time and practice to recognize God's voice. This skill comes easily to some people, while others need time to develop confidence in their ability in this area.

Although people do occasionally report hearing the audible voice of God, most often, when we talk about "hearing the voice of God", we are referring to any number of the ways He communicates with us. Some of the ways that people hear from the Lord are:

- thoughts, ideas, words
- a sense of "knowing" and understanding what He is saying
- dreams, visions
- an audible voice
- a peace we have when we consider what we believe He is showing us
- a revelation while reading the Scriptures
- something spoken to us by someone else

As we step out in faith, acting upon what we believe the Lord has shown us, we begin to recognize the ways He communicates with us. We receive more clarity as He "fine tunes" the discernment we have received. We say in our hearts "Yes! I did hear! That was His voice!"

Almost everyone can relate to times in our lives when we have desperately needed to hear from the Lord. How grateful we have been when we have been able to receive direction and comfort from Him!

- Let the Lord show you creative ways to pray, even though you may have a routine or favorite style of prayer. This can be one of the most meaningful times you spend together!
- Encourage each other by expressing your appreciation for these times of prayer. Share testimonies of answered prayer, and ask caring questions to encourage praying together. (e.g. "When would be a good time for you?")
- Praying together does not eliminate your need for personal prayer time with the Lord. Your private prayer time is your chance to pray in all the ways that you prefer. Praying together may require a lot of compromise in order to reach agreement.
- Choose a time and place.
- Begin with a pattern of prayer, then flow more and more freely.
- Considering both spouse's preferences is they key to agreement on this pattern of prayer.

SESSION TWO, pp. 27-49

SOME TYPES OF PRAYER

As you read the following list, underline some types of prayer that appeal to you. Also underline any types of prayer that the Holy Spirit seems to be encouraging you to try. This will be helpful as you complete your assignments after this Study Guide.

- Listen to the Lord, then share with each other. He has such beautiful and meaningful things to say to you. WE THINK THAT LISTENING IS THE MOST IMPORTANT PART OF PRAYER.
- Incorporate Scripture reading, study, meditation, and memorization.
- Search the Scriptures on a selected topic, then share insights with one another.
- Pray prophetically.
- Pray in tongues
- Praise the Lord, calling Him by His names.
- Take time to repent to the Lord and to one another.
- Thank Him specifically for blessings.
- Intercede for others.
- Discern His will, and then petition Him for your needs.
- Journal what the Lord speaks to each of you during times of "listening prayer". Review these notes periodically.
- Read a devotional book together.
- Ask Him questions.
- Pray spontaneously, out loud throughout the day.
- Just sit and enjoy the Lord's presence together.
- Keep a notebook of prayer needs and requests.
- Be "real" with Him. Tell Him your thoughts and feelings. He cares.
- Read spiritually based books to one another.
- Sing, play instruments, listen to worship music together.
- Fast and pray, as the Lord Leads.
- Skip a meal ... share communion instead.
- Look into the Scriptures, seeking the Lord for revelation (whatever the Lord desires to reveal, or revelation about a decision or a certain topic).
- Let the Lord impress upon you His constant presence and involvement in every aspect of your life. Ask for grace to be increasingly aware of Him.
- Lay hands upon one another, bless one another and pray for specific needs.
- Seek the Lord at the beginning of each year, asking Him to speak to you about the coming season. Keep a record of the things He shows you.

SESSION TWO, pp. 27-49

A WORD TO THE WISE …

Who should lead in prayer? Many say "the man". In fact, some couples or families don't pray together at all because the wife is waiting for her husband to lead. It is wonderful when a husband takes the lead and initiates these times of prayer, but if the wife is stronger in her prayer discipline and motivation, she may be the one to initiate joint times of prayer. The thing that really matters is that couples and families pray together. If a wife says to God "I can't pray with my husband because he won't accept leadership in this area.", I don't believe God says "Oh, I am so sorry. I understand that you can't pray together." I believe He says something like "Don't give up. Keep seeking Me and I will give you creative ways to initiate prayer together."

Whether you are the man or the woman, do whatever you can to make this possible. Keep a positive attitude. Take your spouse's hand and pray a brief prayer, punctuated by an energetic "Amen!". Pray out loud as you receive an email prayer request, asking your spouse to agree with you in prayer. Lay your hand on your spouse's shoulder as they leave for work or a meeting, saying "Lord, I thank you for my spouse and I bless him/her as he/she faces this day. May he/she experience your strength, wisdom, and presence." At night, after turning out the lights, touch your spouse's hand and say "Lord, I am grateful to You for Your love today. Thank you for our marriage. Please forgive us any wrong attitudes and help us to cooperate with Your grace." Short, pleasant prayers lead to more prayers. Short, answered prayers lead to more faith. And, most importantly, prayer that is based on two way conversations with God is based on relationship and it will grow, because listening to God fills our prayers with life.

SESSION TWO, pp. 27-49

INDIVIDUAL ASSIGNMENT #2a

1. Describe your current prayer life as a couple _____

2. How long would you like to pray together? _____ Where? _____

3. What time of day would you prefer to pray with your partner? _____ What is the second best time of day for you to pray with your spouse? _____

4. What types of joint prayer are of most interest to you? _____

5. Here are two sample "Patterns of Prayer" for use during times of prayer together.

PRAYER PATTERN #1	PRAYER PATTERN #2
Worship CD	Sing a worship song
Read passage of Bible to each other	Thanksgiving
Repentance to God and each other	Petition God for personal needs
Time to listen to God	Intercede for the needs of others
Intercession	Time to listen to God

6. List two patterns of prayer to suggest to your partner for your mutual prayer times.

PRAYER PATTERN #1	PRAYER PATTERN #2

CONTINUE SESSION TWO ON PAGE 35

The Intimate Marriage (5)
© 2013 Paraklesis Ministries

SESSION TWO, pp. 27-49

SESSION TWO, pp. 27-49

STUDY GUIDE #2b
JOHARI WINDOW
A TOOL FOR ANALYZING AND IMPROVING COMMUNICATION

Broken relationship and divorce are rampant today. Even couples and families who remain together sometimes live in the same house separated by walls of indifference or outright hostility. Often people who request pre-marriage or marriage ministry have never observed the patterns of healthy communication between loving spouses.

According to a 1989 poll by George Gallup[6,] of those marriages that ended in divorce, "three-fifths … (57%) failed due to poor communication, or to poor conflict resolution skills." It is our opinion that many problems in marriage, even financial difficulties, may be traced back to weaknesses in communication and the resulting unresolved conflicts. Many people rank financial problems high on the list of causes for divorce. Others site sexual dysfunction as a common root of incompatibility. But we find that these dilemmas, as well as other common problems in marriages and families, are often symptoms that stem from lack of communication skills or poor communication practices. Underlying the poor communication skills may be lack of knowledge and/or the need for emotional healing. Many marriages are dissolved on the grounds of "irreconcilable differences" when the real problem was a lack of intimacy due to inability to resolve feelings and conflicts

📖 **"But the wisdom from above is first pure, peaceable, gentle, and easy to be entreated, full of mercy and good fruits, without partiality, and without hypocrisy." (Ja.3:17)**

Good communication, as described in this verse, includes the concept of openness and honesty without hypocrisy. In Vine's Complete Expository Dictionary[7], being "without hypocrisy" is defined as "being without pretense, not play-acting."

SOME SIGNS OF HEALTHY COMMUNICATION: (INTIMACY)
- Open, honest, real
- Both partners feel comfortable sharing feelings
- The feedback given encourages continued intimate expression of feelings
- Both partners are motivated to understand and to listen to each other, as well as to share about themselves
- Conflicts and feelings are resolved regularly
- Words are encouraging, edifying
- Conflict is viewed as an opportunity for personal change and for growth as a couple.

---

[7] Michael J. McManus, <u>Marriage Savers</u>, (Grand Rapids, Michigan: Zondervan Publishing House, 1993) 123
[7] Vine, Unger, and White, 316

SESSION TWO, pp. 27-49

JOHARI WINDOW

The Johari Window is a tool developed by two psychologists, Joseph Luft and Harrington Ingham for the purpose of analyzing communication styles.

By looking at the Johari Window model, you will learn about your communication style and be able to set some goals to grow in this key area of your relationships.

"Think of the whole diagram as representing your total self as you reveal yourself to others. Every relationship you have can be described by a Johari Window and no two will be alike."

Everything there is to know about you is in your Johari Window. Information about you may be in the arena, the blind spot, the mask, or the potential. The amount of information in each "windowpane" will vary with the level of intimacy in each relationship. In a very intimate relationship, the ARENA will hold a lot of information, known to both parties. Information moves from the blind spot, mask, or potential into the arena as the relationship grows and information is shared, perceived, or observed.

ARENA	**BLIND SPOT**
I KNOW	I DON'T KNOW
YOU KNOW	YOU DO KNOW
MASK	**POTENTIAL**
I KNOW	I DON'T KNOW
YOU DON'T KNOW	YOU DON'T KNOW

THINK ABOUT IT…

- If a person has a large *arena* in a certain relationship, they have a lot of insight about themselves (I KNOW) and the other person knows a lot about what they are really like (YOU KNOW).
- If person has a large *blind spot* in a certain relationship, there is a lot that they don't know about themselves (I DON'T KNOW), but there are things the other person does know about them and could tell them about if they would receive input (YOU DO KNOW).
- If a person has a large *mask* in a certain relationship, they may have a lot of knowledge about themselves (I KNOW), but there is a lot that the other person doesn't know about them (YOU DON'T KNOW).
- If a person has a large *potential* in a certain relationship, there is a lot that they don't know about themselves (I DON'T KNOW), and there is a lot the other person doesn't know about them (YOU DON'T KNOW).

SESSION TWO, pp. 27-49

COMMUNICATION STYLES

Remember, it's not likely that a person continually communicates in one style or the other, although one style may be predominant in each relationship. Stress, pressure, time restraints, embarrassment, defensiveness, denial or other factors can all pressure a person not to disclose information or be open to input from others.

IDEAL WINDOW, LARGE ARENA *(trusting, intimate relationship)*

ARENA	**BLIND SPOT**
I KNOW	I DON'T KNOW
YOU KNOW	YOU DO KNOW
MASK	**POTENTIAL**
I KNOW	I DON'T KNOW
YOU DON'T KNOW	YOU DON'T KNOW

* Healthy communication
* Congruent (Thoughts, words, and actions match)
* Balanced
* Various levels of communication, depending upon the relationship desired

<u>INCREASING THE ARENA</u>: Decreasing the blind spot (by receiving input from others) or the mask (by revealing information about yourself to others) will enlarge the arena and increase intimacy. That is, these exchanges of information will place more facts and insights into the arena, the area in which both people are aware of the information.

**All relationships should not be intimate, but a close,
honest relationship with one's mate or family members is
IDEAL!**

SESSION TWO, pp. 27-49

INTERVIEWER
LARGE MASK

(Personal information hidden. Focus is on the other person)

ARENA	BLIND SPOT
I KNOW	I DON'T KNOW
YOU KNOW	YOU DO KNOW

MASK	POTENTIAL
I KNOW	I DON'T KNOW
YOU DON'T KNOW	YOU DON'T KNOW

- Controls conversations by asking lots of questions to keep others talking, or steering the discussion toward topics with which they feel uncomfortable.
- Avoids revealing much about himself/herself.
- Wants to know where others stand before expressing their personal thoughts or feelings.
- Feels insecure.
- Concerned that others will judge them if they know certain information.
- In certain relationships, a large mask is the healthy or necessary choice. (e.g. at work or in an unsafe relationship)

A person with a sad facial expression who says "I am fine!" is not being congruent.

DECREASING THE MASK: A person can decrease their mask by disclosing information about themselves and/or giving feedback to others (exposing their personal thoughts and feelings). We can provide opportunity for a person to decrease a large mask by giving nonjudgemental feedback when information is disclosed. This will provide them an opportunity to be glad that they did share.

SESSION TWO, pp. 27-49

BULL IN THE CHINA SHOP
LARGE BLIND SPOT *(Often unaware of their personal issues.)*

ARENA	BLIND SPOT
I KNOW	I DON'T KNOW
YOU KNOW	YOU DO KNOW
MASK	**POTENTIAL**
I KNOW	I DON'T KNOW
YOU DON'T KNOW	YOU DON'T KNOW

- Insensitive
- Feedback not received
- Reveals and solicits information regardless of the other person's desires.
- They may "execute the messenger". i.e. Their response when others give them feedback is often angry or passionate, and this makes others reluctant to continue to give feedback

DECREASING THE BLIND SPOT: A person with a large blind spot can decrease it by receiving feedback or input about themselves. There is information that we may not be able to learn unless we will receive it from the Holy Spirit or another person. Although it can be humbling to receive from someone else, sometimes this is how God reveals information and understanding to us. When we receive input, even if it doesn't seem to apply, it is important make an effort to respond openly. For example: "You know, I can't really see that at this point, but I will be glad to pray about it and to consider what you said." OR "I don't really see that, can you help me understand what causes you to think that may apply?"

We urge people to focus mainly upon the changes they need to make, but there are times when giving feedback or input can be very valuable to the other person, and to the relationship. If someone close to you has a large Blind Spot, ask them if they would like you to offer some information. Be sensitive and compassionate in your presentation of the information, keeping in mind that you may not be right! Just offer the suggestion, often in the form of a question. (Do you think …?). Then release it! Also consider taking a risk and sharing about your personal struggles or failings. This may open their eyes to their own.

SESSION TWO, pp. 27-49

TURTLE
LARGE POTENTIAL
(Hides information about self. Doesn't seek information about others.)

ARENA	**BLIND SPOT**
I KNOW	I DON'T KNOW
YOU KNOW	YOU DO KNOW
MASK	**POTENTIAL**
I KNOW	I DON'T KNOW
YOU DON'T KNOW	YOU DON'T KNOW

- In a shell"
- Avoids close relationships.
- Very little feedback given or received
- An observer
- Has little insight into themselves
- May not be sensitive to or aware of the feelings and opinions of others.

<u>DECREASING THE POTENTIAL</u>: Prophetic words can reveal information that is in the potential. Trying new things and acting upon prophetic words or counsel can uncover information that is in the potential. Sharing feelings and listening to others attentively can also help to open up the potential and to move information into the arena.

IN SUMMARY:

Making and taking time for relationship is essential. This will be rewarding, as it will increase intimacy, even though it may not be comfortable at first.

By looking at your communication style (see assignment, page 41), you will be able to identify strengths and weaknesses and to take some steps toward an increasingly intimate relationship with your partner, your family or others.

SESSION TWO, pp. 27-49

INDIVIDUAL ASSIGNMENT #2b

1. Johari Window. Fill in the blanks for questions a, c, d, & e with the words <u>Ideal Window</u>, <u>Interviewer</u>, <u>Bull in the China Shop</u> or <u>Turtle</u>.

   a. Most often, in my relationship with my partner, I see myself as a _____ communicator, and my partner as a _____ communicator.

   b. In order to improve my communication with my partner, I will _____
   _____
   _____
   _____

   c. At church, I see myself as a _____ communicator and my partner as a _____ communicator.

   d. In social situations, I see myself as a _____ communicator and my partner as a _____ communicator.

CONTINUE SESSION TWO ON PAGE 43…

The Intimate Marriage (5)
© 2013 Paraklesis Ministries

SESSION TWO, pp. 27-49

SESSION TWO, pp. 27-49

STUDY GUIDE #2c
FEELINGS

You can't live out of your feelings! How many Christians have been given this misleading advice? What this often means is that we are only to feel certain "permissible" feelings, while suppressing all other emotions. While it is true that we are not at liberty to excuse our behaviors by blaming them on our unresolved emotions, it is also true that if we deny our feelings, it is to our own detriment. Feelings that are denied can't be resolved.

Feelings are common to all of us. Denying them stifles the level of intimacy in our relationships. It also leads to destructive relational patterns and personal habits. If we don't admit our feelings and deal with them, the likelihood is that we WILL end up living out of them!

If someone says they don't have feelings, it is likely that they have become accustomed to suppressing their emotions. Later, these feelings probably surface in their behaviors, attitudes, tone of voice, body language, or facial expressions. Unresolved discouragement may cause irritability with others. Accumulated unexpressed anger may cause and irrational overreaction, such as a slammed door or a speeding car. "I don't care!" often becomes a temper tantrum.

"Addictions (which are considered a "disease of the feelings"), road rage, and all kinds of abuse are also common manifestations of unresolved feelings. The victims in these unfortunate situations have not caused the rage, but have become the tragic targets of someone else's runaway emotions. It is important to be aware of our feelings and to resolve them rather than allowing them to build and then to erupt in unhealthy ways and at inopportune times.

People who habitually deny their feelings become "numb", unable to feel the pleasant OR the unpleasant feelings. Others have become so pent-up with emotions that the main feeling they express is anger. In this lesson, you will learn several methods for identifying and resolving feelings.

People often grow up in an environment that discourages healthy communication skills. It is not surprising that many of them employ these same unsuccessful practices in their own marriages and families even though they may have witnessed disastrous results in their family of origin. It may be that they aren't motivated to change, but it is much more likely that they just don't know any other way. The effective communication tools in this workbook will improve relationship skills and introduce healthy patterns that will impact the next generation.

Change is hard work. It takes time, patience, and practice, but it is well worth the effort. People who become accustomed to sharing feelings and resolving them have more intimate and healthy relationships.

SESSION TWO, pp. 27-49

SOME THOUGHTS ABOUT ANGER

Anger can have a wide variety of underlying causes. When a person expresses anger, it is likely that there are additional feelings beneath the anger. For this reason, anger is often called a "surface feeling". In other words, it is on the surface, or it "shows", but it covers over some other feeling(s). It is important for us to know how to get in touch with the deeper feelings so that they can be resolved and communicated in a healthy way.

One classic example of anger as a surface feeling is that of the mother whose child is lost at the shopping mall.

In the first example, when the child is finally returned to the mother, her reaction may be an angry one like this: "Don't you EVER do that to me again!" The child in this case hears the anger, but has no idea of the feelings that lie deeper, beneath the surface. This child may feel ashamed or rejected, or even embarrassed or unloved, especially if others are listening to the angry comment as he is reunited with his mother. It is very likely that this mother's surface anger is covering other more significant and appropriate feelings.

Let's look at a second example of how this incident could be handled in a more constructive manner: This mother may actually feel angry at first, but if she will search beneath the surface, she may find feelings like fear and relief. When she first sees her child, she might hug him and tell him how fearful she felt while he was lost and how relieved she feels to have found him. At the very least, the child will be asked to stay close by in the future. If the child is old enough to have realized that they were disobeying, they may receive a consequence for wandering off. However, they will know that their parent loves them and cares about their well being because of the feelings that were shared with them.

Can you see how the child and parent in the first example could have a damaged relationship and the child and parent in the second example could connect heart to heart as they work through this difficult situation together? Anger can destroy a relationship or it can be a signal that causes someone to dig deeper so that their true emotions can be identified and resolved.

If someone is not able to consistently deal with anger in a healthy way, they may take out their anger on whomever happens to be interacting with them at the moment. It is advisable for them to seek healing ministry in order to resolve the true cause that underlies their anger.

SESSION TWO, pp. 27-49

ONE OF THE MOST INTIMATE FORMS OF COMMUICATION IS THE SHARING OF FEELINGS IN A HEALTHY MANNER

Example A: (Not intimate. Details shared, not feelings.)
Wife: Hi, honey, how was your day at work?
Husband: It was O.K. My boss called another meeting this morning without giving us any notice. I don't know how he expects us to be productive when he keeps doing things like that. I had to get out of there for a while so Joe and I went to lunch at BJ's.

Example B: (Intimate. Feelings, not details, are emphasized.)
Wife: Hi, honey. How was your day at work?
Husband: I felt stressed about an unexpected meeting because I thought I would have to leave some urgent things on my desk. Instead, I put in a quick call to Mel and he stepped in to help. I felt so relieved about that because I knew it would be well covered.

Do you see the difference in the level of intimacy? Both conversations are the same length, but the wife in example B has a much better idea of what her husband's experience was really like. There is a greater level of intimacy and trust in Example B.

The daily emphasis on feelings rather than details adds intimacy to your relationships. Even simple, everyday situations can be communicated in a way that will greatly increase your intimacy and trust level over the years if you are willing to do this. It is not necessary for every relationship to grow to a level of deep intimacy. However, we can intentionally choose to share at a level which increases the level of intimacy and trust in the relationships we desire to strengthen.

USE THE FEELING FORMULA TO IDENTIFY AND TO SHARE FEELINGS:

I feel/felt _____ about _____ because I think/thought _____
          Feeling   Issue   Belief

EXAMPLE: I felt upset about my grade because I thought it was much lower than I deserved.

PEOPLE WHO OFTEN THINK BEFORE THEY FEEL CAN REVERSE THE FEELING FORMULA:

I think/believe that _____ and that makes me feel _____
                Belief about an Issue   Feeling

EXAMPLE: I think that the traffic moves too slowly in this area and it makes me feel frustrated.

At first, it may seem awkward to use a formula to share feelings, but the relational benefits will be well worth the effort required!

SESSION TWO, pp. 27-49

THE FEELING FORMULA EXERCISE
CAN YOU SPOT THE ERRORS IN THESE EXAMPLE FEELING FORMULAS?

Example One: "I feel <u>that</u> it is important to make this decision soon because the deadline is next week."

1. In the case of formula #1, the first blank is filled with "that", which is not a feeling word. This is a common mistake, and it results in the sharing of an opinion rather than sharing feelings. Opinions are interesting. They are informative. But opinions do not lead to a deep intimacy. One of the purposes of using the feeling formula is to increase vulnerability and intimacy. We suggest this alternative to feeling formula #1 above:

FORMULA: "I <u>feel</u> anxious <u>about</u> the decision <u>because</u> I believe that the deadline is next week".

Example Two: "I feel irritated about the schedule because you didn't even offer to help."

2. The only personal pronoun in the feeling formula is the word "I", the person responsible for the feelings. In the second example above, the focus is on the listener rather than on the changes that need to be made by the person who is sharing. We suggest this alternative for the feeling formula #2 above:

FORMULA: "I <u>feel</u> irritated <u>about</u> the schedule <u>because I think</u> I have to do all the work myself."

The benefit of this corrected feeling formula is that it accurately identifies the source of this person's irritation and this gives them the ability to change their feelings by changing their thought. If we use a feeling formula that blames our feelings on someone else (as the example, above, "you didn't even offer to help."), then we are trapped in those unpleasant emotions until and unless the other person changes. If they are causing our feelings, then they must change in order for our feelings to be changed. We give the other person control over our emotional well being! If they don't change, then we will be miserable. Let's not give that much control to someone else.

3. Please list your three greatest fears:

　　　　a. _____

　　　　b. _____

　　　　c. _____

SESSION TWO, pp. 27-49

FEELINGS LIST

The feelings at the top of each column are somewhat similar to the feelings in the column.

Happy	Sad	Caring	Angry	Afraid	Confused
Ecstatic	Abused	Secure	Bitter	Alarmed	Bewildered
Elated	Defeated	Firm	Defiant	Fearful	Immobilized
Delighted	Depressed	Loving	Disgusted	Horrified	Torn
Close	Drained	Powerful	Enraged	Panicky	Trapped
Great	Distant	Loved	Furious	Petrified	Troubled
Amused	Grief-stricken	Strong	Mad	Terrified	Pulled apart
Eager	Hopeless	Respected	Rejected	Apprehensive	Disturbed
Cheerful	Lonely	Affectionate	Seething	Impatient	Disorganized
Grateful	Miserable	Carefree	Agitated	Insecure	Blocked
Joyful	Burdened	Comforted	Annoyed	Threatened	Misunderstood
Open	Discouraged	Compassionate	Envious	Uneasy	Mixed-up
Proud	Distressed	Confident	Irritated	Worried	Frustrated
Surprised	Down	Empathetic	Edgy	Inadequate	Undecided
Warm	Guilty	Proud	Pent-up	Anxious	Uncomfortable
Hopeful	Helpless	Sympathetic	Grumpy	Nervous	Bothered
Cooperative	Ashamed	Trusting	Resentful	Tense	Puzzled
Glad	Bad	Calm	Disappointed	Timid	Uncertain

Feeling Formula Guidelines

1. "I" is the only person in the feeling formula.
2. "I" am responsible for my own feelings.
3. "Like" and "that" are not feelings. E.g. Don't say "I feel like…"
4. Don't settle for surface feelings or dishonest feelings that "sound better". Be searching and fearless, identifying all of the true feelings evoked.
5. Include all three parts of the feeling formula.
6. Remember that the "about" should be brief, about 4-5 words.
7. Take strong feelings to the Lord first.
8. You may have to repent for your feelings and the beliefs and attitudes that they reflect, but your feelings are accurate. Thoughts and opinions may be wrong.
9. Don't use the feeling formula to manipulate
10. Ask the Holy Spirit to reveal all of the feelings about a particular issues.

The Intimate Marriage (5)
© 2013 Paraklesis Ministries

SESSION TWO, pp. 27-49

INDIVIDUAL ASSIGNMENT #2c

USING THE FEELING FORMULA

It's time to identify feelings using the feeling formula. Please use a pencil as you fill in the blanks below. You may want to refer to the list of feelings on the previous page in order to be accurate in identifying your feelings. After you write each Feeling Formula, please check it with the Feeling Formula Guidelines on the previous page and make any necessary corrections on this copy.

EXAMPLE:
I feel (annoyed) about (raking leaves) because I think (it is a waste of time).

1. I feel (am feeling, felt) _____

   about ..... _____drinking Coke_____

   Because I think (believe, thought) _____

2. I feel (am feeling, felt) _____

   about ..... _____

   because I think (believe, thought) _____

3. I feel (am feeling, felt) _____

   about _____

   because I think (believe, thought) _____

4. I feel (am feeling, felt) _____

   about _____

   because I think (believe, thought) _____

5. I feel (am feeling, felt) _____

   about _____

   because I think (believe, thought) _____

IMPORTANT ASSIGNMENT
Using the Feeling Formula, begin to journal the negative feelings that you are experiencing. Write three Feeling Formulas per day for 21 days.
You can use the form on the next page for a master if you like.

SESSION TWO, pp. 27-49

FEELING FORMULA WORKSHEET
Skip "methods used to resolve" until you have studied pp.55-58.

> Example: I feel .... (annoyed)
> about .... (raking leaves)
> because I think ...(it is a waste of time.)

1. I feel (am feeling, felt) _____

    about _____

    because I think (believe, thought) _____

    Methods used to resolve this feeling: See p.56. List #'s here: _____

2. I feel (am feeling, felt) _____

    about ..... _____

    because I think (believe, thought) _____

    Methods used to resolve this feeling: See p.53. List #'s here: _____

3. I feel (am feeling, felt) _____

    about ..... _____

    because I think (believe, thought) _____

    Methods used to resolve this feeling: See p.56. List #'s here: _____

4. I feel (am feeling, felt) _____

    about DRINKING COKE ..... _____

    because I think (believe, thought) _____

    Methods used to resolve this feeling: See p.56. List #'s here: _____

5. I feel (am feeling, felt) _____

    about ..... _____

    because I think (believe, thought) _____

    Methods used to resolve this feeling: See p.56. List #'s here: _____

6. I feel (am feeling, felt) _____

    about ..... _____

    because I think (believe, thought) _____

    Methods used to resolve this feeling: See p.56. List #'s here: _____

The Intimate Marriage (5)
© 2013 Paraklesis Ministries

SESSION TWO, pp. 27-49

SECOND JOINT SESSION, pp.51-52

SECOND JOINT SESSION

Chose a location in which you can be alone and in which you both feel comfortable sharing intimately with one another. Take a few moments together to prepare the room if necessary. Some couples enjoy soft music, candles, and refreshments. Make the atmosphere pleasant and conducive to a special time together during each of your joint sessions.

OPEN IN PRAYER: Invite the Holy Spirit to lead the session and submit to Him. Express your needs and the desires of your heart for this session.

1. Alternate reading aloud to one another: "Keys to Intimacy", below. Pause after each point to ask one another's forgiveness and extend forgiveness as necessary. Because you are still on first phase, avoid delving into deeply controversial issues at this point. Instead, ask forgiveness and extend forgiveness to one another and set a goal to work through the issues with your minister's assistance.

KEYS TO INTIMACY

a) <u>Be honest.</u> In order to be intimate, people need to be honest with each other. If a person's communication is honest and congruent, their words, feelings, actions, facial expressions, and body language will all agree. If one or more of these elements do not correlate, unhealthy communication will result. If you have ever replied "I am fine!" when you were really thinking "I am angry!", it is likely that your facial expression revealed your true feelings.

b) <u>Be open</u>. Share daily about things you have experienced, even if they seem insignificant to you. Share willingly. Be vulnerable and courageous. The enemy does not want intimacy in your relationship and may bring pressure against you when you try to be open. Don't cooperate with the enemy! Don't expect your partner to drag things out of you. It is your responsibility to be intimate with them and their responsibility to be intimate with you. In codependent relationships, people often feel responsible for each other rather than developing their own character and skills.

c) <u>Be direct.</u> Make specific requests and give your partner the freedom to say "yes" or "no". Hinting, nagging, and name-dropping are forms of manipulation. Although learning to discipline your tongue is essential to avoiding this type of control, trusting the Lord is the key to breaking this habit.

d) <u>Keep your word.</u> It is better to say "No" or "I won't be able to do it until _____ " than to say "Yes", but not mean it and not follow through. A false "Yes" destroys trust. It may postpone conflict and make things seem easier for the moment, but it will definitely not prevent conflict.

e) <u>Make good eye contact</u>. Give your full attention to the other person.

f) <u>Be a safe place for the other person</u>. Give good feedback. Encourage open sharing. Share about your personal feelings and thoughts also.

SECOND JOINT SESSION, pp.51-52

      g) <u>Avoid these communication snares</u>:
- a. Assuming
- b. Judging
- c. Speaking hurtful words
- d. Interrupting
- e. Insisting upon agreement
- f. Poor listening: thinking of your next statement as they are talking
- g. Bringing up mistakes from the past that have already been dealt with
- h. Communicating intimate details to others

      h) <u>Be encouraged!</u> It does become easier with time. Intimacy is a skill that requires the heartfelt cooperation of both partners.

2. What is one sign of healthy communication (See page 35) in which you would like to grow as a couple: ._____

3. Refer to Individual Assignment on page 33.
   - Agree on a time that you plan to pray together.
   - Agree on the place you will pray.
   - Agree on the length of time you will pray (Choose the shorter time at first).
   - Share Patterns of Prayer that each of you developed. Select the first two patterns of Prayer that you want to try during your times of prayer together. Write those patterns in the tables below.

PRAYER PATTERN #1	PRAYER PATTERN #2

4. Refer to your Individual Assignment on page 48 and share feeling formula #1 with each other. (This will be a pleasant feeling formula about drinking Coke.)

5. Husband (or fiancée): Share with your wife (or fiancée) one thing that she could do that would make it easier for you to share your feelings with her.

6. Wife (or fiancée): Share with your husband (or fiancée) one thing that he could do that would make it easier for you to share your feelings with him.

CLOSE IN PRAYER

SESSION THREE pp. 55-67

SESSION THREE
Study Guide #3a: Resolving Feelings 55
Study Guide #3b: Feedback 61
Study Guide #3c: Healthy Communication Pattern 63
Study Guide #3d: Giving and Receiving Input 65
INDIVIDUAL ASSIGNMENTS #3a,b,c,d 59,62,64,67
THIRD JOINT SESSION 69

<u>IF YOU ARE COMPLETING THIS AS A SELF HELP WORKBOOK:</u>

3. Each person should complete all reading and answer all questions on pages 55-67. **Highlight or underline** significant points as you read. Please fill in every blank and answer all questions, as you will need these answers for your joint sessions.

4. Within 1-2 weeks, on the date you set for your joint session (see schedule on page 7), meet with your spouse/fiancée to complete together the Joint Session #3 on page 69.

<u>IF YOU ARE RECEIVING MINISTRY:</u>

c) Complete all reading and answer all questions on pages 55-67. **Highlight or underline** significant points as you read. Please fill in every blank and answer all questions, as you will need these answers for your ministry session.

d) When assigned, meet with your spouse/fiancée to complete together the Joint Session #3 on page 69

The Intimate Marriage (5)
© 2013 Paraklesis Ministries

SESSION THREE pp. 55-67

SESSION THREE pp. 55-67

STUDY GUIDE #3a
RESOLVING FEELINGS

WE ARE RESPONSIBLE FOR OUR FEELINGS

Feelings may be pleasant or unpleasant, healthy or destructive, but they are common to all of us. Even people who say they don't have many feelings may behave in certain ways because of unexpressed/unresolved feelings! Unhealed hurts and other unresolved feelings become a part of our personality, affecting our personal well-being as well as our relationships. Most of us have heard the expression "Hurt people hurt people."[8] It is important to resolve our feelings so that our hearts are at peace and we are able to avoid the harm that unresolved feelings can cause in a relationship. We'll take some time now to discuss how to deal with the kinds of feelings that require resolution.

📖 **"There is that speaketh like the piercings of a sword: but the tongue of the wise is health."** (Pr.12:18)

It's not acceptable to be ruled by our feelings, (e.g. to treat others unkindly or to speak hurtful words because we <u>feel</u> irritable!) It is possible, with God's help, for feelings to be resolved, even if the other person is not able to repent or to change.

📖 **"A good man out of the good treasure of his heart bringeth forth that which is good; and an evil man out of the evil treasure of his heart bringeth forth that which is evil: for of the abundance of his heart, his mouth speaketh."** (Lu.6:45)

The attitudes of our heart will be reflected in our communication regardless of the words we choose. Anger, judgment, unforgiveness, and other similar feelings often mask deeper emotions. However, if we take these "surface" feelings to the Lord first, He can free us to relate to others in an intimate, godly way. (Psalm 59)

DO YOU KNOW THAT OUR FEELINGS OFTEN COME FROM OUR OWN THOUGHTS?!

📖 **"For as he thinketh in his heart, so is he."** (Pr.23:7a)

Here is an example of how our feelings may change when we change the thought:

I <u>feel</u> worried **about** the finances **because** I think I've never been any good with money.

VS:

I <u>feel</u> optimistic **about** the finances **because** I believe the Lord is giving me wisdom through the counsel being received.

---

[8] **Sandra D. Wilson, <u>Hurt People Hurt People</u>,** (Nashville, Tennessee: Thomas Nelson Publishers, 1993)

The Intimate Marriage (5)

SESSION THREE pp. 55-67

It is very liberating to realize that we are capable of resolving our feelings. We can live in peace if we understand how not to give control of our emotions to someone else. For example, if we are shamed by a grade school teacher, humiliated in front of our class, we may have the normal, painful feelings that can accompany that type of hurt. However, in the days and even years following that hurt, if we don't forgive and we don't receive healing, the hurts are buried in our hearts. When hurts are buried, they are "buried alive". We may not be mindful that they are there, but they become a part of our personality and we may notice the symptoms that arise if someone gets too close to the previous hurt. In this example, if someone corrects us publically or gives us valid input, we may feel defensive. If our boss tries to give us suggestions, we may overreact and take their comments personally instead of looking at them from a professional perspective in order to improve our performance in the workplace. It was the shameful humiliation by the teacher that generated the original hurtful feelings. However, at some point after that experience, the hurtful feelings were no longer due to the experience. They were produced and sustained by the thoughts we had about the experience. For example, we may think "Authority figures do not have my best interests at heart." "I am no good at public speaking." "It is better for me to be quiet than to say the wrong thing." If we acknowledge that it is our own thought that is generating the pain rather than the memory of what was done to us, we realize that whether the teacher ever apologized or recognized their mistake, we are still able to be free. As we forgive that teacher and then confess and receive forgiveness for our own ungodly thinking, we are positioned to receive God's healing.

> ### FOUR WAYS TO RESOLVE FEELINGS
>
> 1. At times, it is adequate to identify the feelings, to forgive and repent as necessary, and to replace the thought with a godly one.
>
> 2. It is often helpful to set one or two goals that will help you to resolve the feelings and, at times, to prevent the situation from recurring.
>
> 3. At other times, you may want to ask your fiancée or your spouse for help with an issue that causes you unpleasant feelings.
>
> 4. Sometimes, feelings may be more difficult to resolve, requiring a specific healing touch from the Lord.
>
>   📖 **"Come unto Me, all ye that labour and are heavy laden and I will give you rest."** Mt. 11:28

SESSION THREE pp. 55-67

We are responsible for our feelings, even if we believe that we are innocent in a situation. Perhaps someone has hurt us and they are not repentant. We are still not excused to entertain (i.e. to hold on to) the hurt and live out of that. We need to pray through until we have been healed. Many of us know people who, when they are offended, become embittered and unforgiving. They ruminate on the offenses, repeatedly mulling them over in their minds, sometimes even becoming distant from God. It is for this reason that Deuteronomy 29:18 warns against taking up offenses. The Lord desires to provide healing at the time of offense and to prevent the bitterness from taking root.

"Surely he hath borne our griefs and carried our sorrows…" (Is. 53:4a)

On the cross, Jesus bore all our sorrows so that we wouldn't have to carry them. Max Lucado addresses this issue in his book, When God Whispers Your Name:[9] He describes taking our bag full of "stones" (i.e. "feelings" like rejection, regret, etc.) to the Lord:

> Jesus says he is the solution for weariness of soul. Go to him. Be honest with him….He's just waiting for you to ask him for help…. Go ahead. You'll be glad you did. (Those near to you will be glad as well … it's hard to throw stones when you've left your sack at the cross.)

"For as the sufferings of Christ abound in us, so our consolation also aboundeth by Christ."   (2Co.1:5)

Jesus, who bore our suffering on the cross, is our consolation. Chester and Betsy Kylstra describe a Holy Spirit directed method of healing in their book Restoring the Foundations.[10] They refer to Psalm 142 as a Biblical pattern for "pouring out our complaint" to God[11] in preparation for healing. According to the Kylstra's:

> David, the great psalmist, gives us numerous examples, all signposts leading in the same direction: taking the innermost issues of our hearts to God. His message is unmistakable: **Be real with God**. Pour out your heart to Him.

In Psalm 142, David is "real" with God. He "pours out his complaint to Him". This is an excellent example of the intimacy in his relationship with the Lord. In Psalm 142, verse three, you will find a key to this process. It states that God sees the path on which we walk, and He even sees the snare that has been set for us by the enemy. Sometimes when we go to God and pour out to him our complaints, He clarifies the plan of the enemy for us and we become compelled not to cooperate with the kingdom of darkness. Instead of the temptation toward self pity, bitterness, or any other plan the enemy had set before us, we are then free to follow the plan of God.

Holy Spirit led healing may be used to deal with current hurts, but it is also effective in resolving hurts from the past, even hurts from childhood. However, people who have experienced significant traumas may need to receive specific counseling or ministry to deal with these issues.

---

[9] **Max Lucado, When God whispers Your Name (USA: Word Publishing, 1994) 121-2**
[10] **Betsy and Chester Kylstra, Restoring the Foundations (Santa Rosa Beach, Florida: Proclaiming His Word, Inc., 1994) 136**
[11] **Kylstras credit their missionary friend, Steve Cobb, with this application**

SESSION THREE pp. 55-67

One common misunderstanding in the area of dealing with past hurts is caused by what we believe is a misinterpretation of Philippians 3:13, in which Paul says "Forgetting those things which are behind…". What he's saying is that those things are so healed that I no longer "remember" them in the way I used to see them. They have now become stepping stones, a part of my testimony. According to Dr. James Friesen, a well known psychologist, hurts which have not been healed are not in the past. They are current issues, affecting our personality and hindering our relationships. If people are pressured to "just get over it", they may be denied an opportunity to be healed and restored. Hurts must be admitted and dealt with in order to be healed.

Of special note is the experience that many who have received the healing ministry of the Holy Spirit will verify. Once a person has received healing from a painful experience, he/she no longer "remembers" the incident in the same way. Having received God's comfort and the revelation of His perspective on the incident, they "remember" it differently. Then, they are truly able to "forget" the old perception because they now have a new way of looking at the memory.

Here is a prayer outline that you can use to pray through hurts and other feelings that need a healing touch from the Lord. It is based upon Chester and Betsy Kylstra's soul spirit hurt healing prayer in Restoring the Foundations. We share it here with their permission:

1. Pour out all your feelings to the Lord. He cares. He understands.
2. Take the feelings to the cross. Jesus has already borne them.
3. Forgive all those the Holy Spirit brings to mind, including yourself, if necessary
4. Repent specifically to the Lord (and to others, unless it would cause them unnecessary pain) for all that He shows you.
5. Ask Jesus to show you where He was at that time, then ask Him to heal your heart.
6. Watch and listen as the Lord restores and heals your heart.[12] He may show you a picture, a moving picture, and/or speak words that bring healing. If He shows you something or speaks something that does not seem to bring healing from the situation, ask Him about it until you understand what He is saying to you and you receive your healing.

Suggestions: As you pray through additional hurts, keep a record of these intimate times with the Lord in a journal. Be sure to request ministry for significant unresolved issues.

---

[12] **Some hurts may require specific ministry by your pastor or another counselor**

SESSION THREE pp. 55-67

INDIVIDUAL ASSIGNMENT #3a

1. Look at the three fears you listed on page 46 and ask the Lord to show you the memory in which one of them originated. Pray through that memory for healing, using the six steps on page 58. Write out step six (the healing words/pictures) below.

2. How do our thoughts affect our feelings? (Page 55)

3. Read and meditate upon Psalm 142. Explain verse 3 in your own words.

4. Name four ways to resolve (i.e. to "take responsibility") for feelings (see page 56).

   a.

   b.

   c.

   d.

SESSION THREE pp. 55-67

SESSION THREE pp. 55-67

STUDY GUIDE 3b
FEEDBACK

"I will always love you." … "I can tell you anything." … "There's no one like you." … These aren't quotes from a Hollywood movie! If you are engaged or married, it is likely that you have made similar statements to your partner. Perhaps they have said similar things to you. Why is it, then, that so many couples who begin with a beautiful bond, find that the passion and the closeness they once felt in their relationship has diminished over time? Often, the answer is found in their lack of certain communication skills, such as feedback. In this lesson, we will address the topic of using "feedback", a very powerful tool, capable of strengthening the level of intimacy in a relationship.

Many people want to be the kind of person in whom others can confide. They say they want people to be "real" with them. However, if they don't know how to respond when someone shares vulnerably, they will not experience the intimacy they desire. Incorporating the habit of giving good feedback can make a significant difference in the level of communication. While healthy feedback is an important part of any relationship, it is especially effective in a marriage where trust is vital.

WHAT IS FEEDBACK?

Feedback is your initial response to what someone else shares with you. When people say "You don't listen to me.", they are not saying "You don't hear me." They are actually saying something like "You don't respond in a way that makes me feel understood." Feedback can cause people to feel "heard" because it expresses understanding. It assures the other person that we have heard them and that we are giving importance to what they have shared.

WHEN TO GIVE FEEDBACK

You may give feedback after someone shares their feelings, asks a question, or shares their opinion or their preferences with you. Some conflicts arise because of a lack of feedback. In this case the person who is supposed to be listening is actually just thinking about what they are going to say next. As soon as the first person shares, instead of giving good feedback, the second person immediately shares their own views, often differing from the first person's views. Giving good feedback may prevent a conflict in this example, as it will express your understanding of what the first person shared. After you give feedback to them, you may share your views.

HOW TO GIVE FEEDBACK
REMEMBER TO:

- Listen without interrupting (Ja.1:19 "Let every man be swift to hear, slow to speak." The "hear" in this verse implies to "listen so that you have deep understanding".)
- Hold your opinion! You are not responsible for fixing the feelings.

SESSION THREE pp. 55-67

THEN:

- "Rejoice with those that do rejoice, weep with those who weep." Ro.12:15. One of the most common mistakes we make is to reverse this Scripture. We often try to cheer up those who are sad or upset. We also may tend to throw a wet blanket on those who are excited about a possibility. These responses may generate feelings of being misunderstood. Instead of encouragement, if we will express compassion for the one who is grieved or in emotional pain, we will not increase their pain. Instead, we will give them a safe place to explore and express their true feelings.
- Repeat what they have shared, in their own words (this is called reflective feedback). Be sure to pay attention to any feelings words they use and to reflect this emotion in your feedback. (e.g. So you are feeling fearful?)
- Speak words which bless. (Pr.18:21)
- Show kindness and acceptance.
- Do respond to any requests for help.
- Ask caring questions (How do you feel about that? Could you tell me more about that? Is there anything I can do? What do you think you need to do?)
- "Press them to the Lord." 📖 **"In me is thine help." (Ho.13:9b)**

INDIVIDUAL ASSIGNMENT #3b
TROUBLESHOOTING: Common Communication Blocks

This exercise is a reminder that this process is all about focusing mainly on the changes that "I" need to make personally, rather than "working on my partner". People who say that their partner will not share with them should consider that "I" may be a part of the problem and begin to look for changes "I" can make. Sometimes people don't share much with us because we are often trying to "fix" their problem and they are just looking for someone who cares. Sometimes people don't share because we aren't giving good feedback and they don't feel safe opening up. People who say that their partner doesn't listen to them should look at whether "I" am communicating well by using the feeling formula, which is brief and right to the point. It is hard to listen when someone consistently talks much more than they listen. It is hard to listen and to understand when someone rambles. The feeling formula goes right to the heart of the matter. Feedback equals good listening. And good communication feels like love.

1. What did you learn about yourself as you read the paragraph above? _____

2. What can you do to increase the level of intimacy in conversations with your partner? _____

SESSION THREE pp. 55-67

STUDY GUIDE #3c
HEALTHY COMMUNICATION PATTERN

Now that you have learned the Feeling Formula, the feeling resolution methods, and feedback, you are ready to use a communication tool called the Healthy Communication Pattern. This tool will help you and your partner to communicate accurately in a safe environment, increasing the level of intimacy and connectedness in the relationship. If you are on First Phase at this point, use this pattern to share lighthearted feelings. This is good practice and will help you to use the pattern for heavier matters on the later phases. If you have written out the resolution for a negative feeling formula, you could also share this feeling formula as a part of a Healthy Communication Pattern on phase one.

WHAT IS THE HEALTHY COMMUNICATION PATTERN?

1. Person #1 Shares their feelings, using the Feeling Formula.

2. Person #1 Takes responsibility for the feelings they shared.

3. Person #2 Gives good feedback.

THEN, if Person #2 has something that they would like to share, they begin with step #1, sharing their feeling formula and then taking responsibility before Person #2 gives good feedback.

Notice that Person #2 does not say anything until after person #1 has shared their feelings and also taken responsibility.

If you are talking to someone who does not know these skills, you may improve the intimacy level of selected relationships by

- Give priority to sharing your feelings, thoughts, and experiences with them. This will establish that you are a safe place, a person who is not afraid to be real and to be vulnerable.

- Encourage them to share and to take responsibility for their feelings by asking 1-2 caring questions. For example:
  - How did that make you feel?
  - What did you think about it?
  - What do you think would help?

- Avoid trying to "fix" their feelings. You might occasionally ask if you could help, soliciting their agreement before stepping in and honoring their boundary if they say "no" and do not accept your help.

The Intimate Marriage (5)
© 2013 Paraklesis Ministries

SESSION THREE pp. 55-67

INDIVIDUAL ASSIGNMENT #3c

1. Select two Feeling Formulas from your journal that you would like to share with your partner and record them below. Be sure that you have also written out your method(s) for taking responsibility for these feelings.

   a. If you are on first phase, you may need to write out two new (lighthearted) ones that you can share with your partner. For example:

   FEELING FORMULA: I felt satisfied about supper tonight because I thought the recipe was difficult but it turned out very well.

   b. When "taking responsibility" for a lighthearted Feeling Formula, write out your plan for continuing to experience this pleasant feeling. For example:

   TAKING RESPONSIBILITY: From now on, when I try a new recipe, I think I will expect the best and enjoy making it.

   c. If you are on first phase, and you are meeting with a minister, you may select two of the more negative Feeling Formulas from your journal, as you will be able to share these during your session, when your minister is present to help walk you through these steps. Be sure to resolve these feelings <u>before</u> sharing them in your session.

2. FIRST FEELING FORMULA:

   a. I felt/feel _____

   b. About _____

   c. Because I think/thought/believed _____
   _____
   _____

   TAKING RESPONSIBILITY (Apply and write out some or all of the steps on p. 56. Use separate paper if need be.)
   _____
   _____

3. SECOND FEELING FORMULA:

   a. I felt/feel _____

   b. About _____

   c. Because I think/thought/believed _____
   _____
   _____

   TAKING RESPONSIBILITY(Apply and write out some or all of the steps on p. 56.)
   _____
   _____

SESSION THREE pp. 55-67

STUDY GUIDE #3d
GIVING AND RECEIVING INPUT

WHAT IS INPUT?
For our purposes, input can be defined as

- A positive or negative impression

- About you or your actions

- That another person shares with you

RECEIVING INPUT
📖 "God resisteth the proud, but giveth grace unto the humble."   (James 4:6b)

Most of us have a tendency to resist change, especially personal change. We may find change particularly difficult if it is someone else points out our need for change! However, we know from our study of God's purpose for marriage (p.14) that change is a part of His plan for us, and that He often uses our partner in the process. It is important to be able to receive constructive input, to be able to ask for input, and, when a compliment is offered, to receive it graciously also.

📖 "Am I therefore become your enemy because I tell you the truth?"   (Ga.4:16)

Resist the urge to defend yourself when suggestions are offered. Listen carefully for information that <u>does</u> apply to you. Don't disregard <u>all</u> the advice just because a portion of it is not relevant, in your opinion.

Our partner is in the unique position of seeing us when we are most "off guard". They often observe patterns in us that we may be unable to detect on our own. We need their input in order to see what is in our blind spots. When we learn to receive their input, our spiritual maturity is enhanced and the relationship is strengthened.

FOR SPECIAL CONSIDERATION
When our spouse (or anyone else, for that matter) explains their perspective of something we did or said, and we don't agree, we have a choice. We can defend ourselves and try to explain away the differences. Or, we can receive their input and reply with humility. For example, we might say "Thank you for helping me to understand what you experienced. My motive for saying (or doing) what I did was "……", but I can see that it did not come across that way. Will you please forgive me for this?" We can express a lot of love by showing respect for their feelings and compassion for what they experienced. Then, if need be, we can try to communicate again, mindful of what we have just learned about our partner.

The Intimate Marriage (5)
© 2013 Paraklesis Ministries

SESSION THREE pp. 55-67

GIVING INPUT

📖 "Search me, O God, and know my heart: try me and know my thoughts: And see if there be any wicked way in me, and lead me in the way everlasting." (Ps.139:23-24)

We strongly encourage couples not to focus on each other's need for improvement (codependency) but to dwell primarily on the changes they need to make personally. Be quick to encourage and compliment one another. Occasionally, you may decide that you would like to give your partner some input. Check with the Lord first. Avoid the temptation to control. If your heart is clear and your motives are good, wait for the right time. Then proceed, usually beginning by asking your partner if they would like your input, always being sensitive to their feelings.

Sometimes it's easier to make a point with someone by sharing our own similar experience. For example, if we acknowledge that a comparable event caused us to experience some fear, they may see that they can relate … if, in fact, they can.

📖 "Brethren, if a man is overtaken in a fault, ye which are spiritual, restore such an one in a spirit of meekness; considering thyself, lest thou also be tempted." (Ga.6:1)

Give input with a gentle attitude and a humble heart, considering your own faults and weaknesses. Remember that your perception may not be correct!

An effective means of offering input is a feeling formula with resolution.

If you do give constructive input, we suggest that you offer it for their consideration, then quickly release it. The Holy Spirit can handle the rest!

Although some of us are in the habit of giving input when we are displeased about something, it is important to develop the habit of sharing encouraging input regularly.

Praise your partner for specific godly qualities. Some examples:

A nice compliment, but not the best type of input:
"You're such a good wife."

Great, specific input:
" I really appreciate the way you stopped what you were doing and came to give me a kiss when I came home. I felt so loved."

4rrt'FOOD FOR THOUGHT:
DO YOU GIVE THE KIND OF INPUT YOU LIKE TO RECEIVE?

SESSION THREE pp. 55-67

INDIVIDUAL ASSIGNMENT #3d

1. When giving input, remember:

2. How do you feel and how do you respond when your partner tries to give you input?

3. Please set a goal that will help you to respond in a more constructive way when your partner gives you input.

SESSION THREE pp. 55-67

THIRD JOINT SESSION

OPEN IN PRAYER
Express to the Lord the desires of your heart for this time together.

1. SHARE with each other about the hurt for which you received ministry. (See page 59, #1). Be sure to share the healing which you received as you prayed through each hurt. Practice good feedback skills when it is your turn to listen. (see page 61-62, feedback)

2. ASK the Lord to show you how this fear/hurt was hindering the intimacy in your relationship with your fiancée or spouse. Ask Him to show you the ways the healing will be a blessing in your relationship with your partner. Write the answer here, then share it with one another:

3. TAKE TURNS using the Healthy Communication Pattern (Page 63). CAUTION: On Phase One, when the emphasis is on your personal development, share resolved feelings and issues that are necessary for your daily life together. Avoid bringing up heavy issues or unresolved past hurts, as these will require greater skill and should be reserved for Phase Two. You may also want to have a minister present to assist if you have difficult issues to resolve.

    a. Partner #1, Share a feeling formula (We suggest using one of the **RESOLVED** Feeling Formulas on page 64) with your spouse. Immediately: Take responsibility for any feelings that you share.

    b. Partner #2, Listen, without interrupting, then gives good feedback, according to the guidelines on page 61-62.

    c. Now, repeat this exercise, but take alternate roles as Person #1 and Person #2.

    d. Repeat this exercise on a regular basis, until you are able to use the Healthy Communication Pattern easily. You should be able to do this in three sentences. Person #1 shares a Feeling Formula and then takes responsibility for the feelings. Person #2 gives good feedback. After your Healthy Communication Patterns, each of you will have a basic understanding of your partner's views and feelings. At that point, you can just freely share about the topic.

4. LOOK OVER the topics you have covered during this session. Take turns repenting to one another and forgiving one another in any area the Holy Spirit reveals to you.

5. CLOSE IN PRAYER

SESSION #4, pp. 73 - 82

SESSION FOUR
Study Guide #4a: Codependency 73-75
Study Guide #4b: Disagreements and Differences 77-79
Study Guide #4c: Amends.. 81-82
Study Guide #4d: Restoration 82
INDIVIDUAL ASSIGNMENTS #4a,b,c,d 74,79,82
FOURTH JOINT SESSION 83-84

IF YOU ARE COMPLETING THIS AS A SELF HELP WORKBOOK:
1. Each person should complete all reading and answer all questions on pages 73-82. **Highlight or underline** significant points as you read. Please fill in every blank and answer all questions, as you will need these answers for your joint sessions.
2. Within 1-2 weeks, on the date you set for your joint session (see schedule on page 7), meet with your spouse/fiancée to complete together the Joint Session #4 on pages 83-84.

IF YOU ARE RECEIVING MINISTRY:
1. Complete all reading and answer all questions on pages 73-82 **Highlight or underline** significant points as you read. Please fill in every blank and answer all questions, as you will need these answers for your ministry session.
2. When assigned, meet with your spouse/fiancée to complete together the Joint Session #4 on pages 83-84

The Intimate Marriage (5)
© 2013 Paraklesis Ministries

SESSION #4, pp. 73 - 82

STUDY GUIDE #4a
CODEPENDENCY: GOD ISN'T IN IT

People often ask us what we see as the most common problem in marriages. We quickly reply "Codependency". In the 1990's, there were a number of books written on codependency and we learned from them but found them hard to summarize into a handful of basic principles. In this teaching on codependency, you will learn a simple and very practical description of this basic relational dysfunction, which is capable of sabotaging a marriage or any other relationship. Codependency is often the reason that people fall away or backslide in their relationships with God and others. When two people are looking to each other for needs that can only be met by God, they have removed Him from the center of their relationship. In other words "God is not in" these relationships, as each person depends on their natural skills and reacts to the other based on their perceived needs.

In his book, The Spiritual Man, Watchman Nee explains that all affection should be directed through God. We agree! And we say that all relationships should be directed through God.

In a codependent relationship, each person **reacts** to the other. This causes an inevitable downward spiral toward the lowest common denominator in their relationship. No relationship is stagnant. Each one is moving in either a positive or negative direction over time. Criticisms, negative opinions, and feelings can flow back and forth in an endless stream, as resentment and unforgiveness mount. Manipulation and control are commonplace. The blame game is a familiar crutch. Some of the underlying thoughts are "You aren't meeting my needs." OR "I only do that because he/she does this." "You make me feel …" Yes, in the immediate, someone's choices can cause us pain. However, as time passes, the pain is no longer caused by what happened…or didn't happen…the pain is then caused by what we think/believe about what happened. We are responsible for how we feel because we have a choice about how we think.

In a codependent marriage, a spouse can sit through a marriage weekend hearing everything their partner needs to correct, in denial of their own need for change. Perhaps you are beginning to identify some of these patterns in yourself. When our family received counseling, I viewed a movie about a dysfunctional family several times, each time identifying another family member's role, but only noting my own dysfunction after seeing the film a number of times. I was so focused on everyone else's roles that I was in denial of my own. This is typical of codependency, where two needy people are trying to get the other person to meet their needs. Author Jack Frost described it as "Two ticks and no dog." Both partners in this relationship are endeavoring to get what they need from the other person. The illustration to the right depicts this type of relationship:

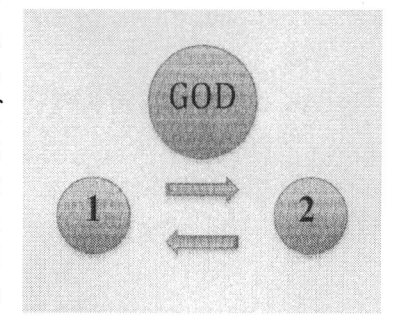

SESSION #4, pp. 73 - 82

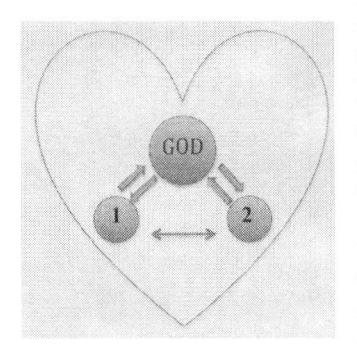

In a healthy relationship, each person **responds** to the Lord and relates to the other person out of the knowledge that they know that they are loved and that all of their needs are known and met by God. The diagram to the left illustrates this type of relationship. Each person is whole. They have integrity. They are congruent. In other words, their thoughts, feelings, and actions match. This enables them to be intimate and to develop genuine relationships. In a conflict or unpleasant conversation, they are able to lean on God and to respond with wisdom and compassion. They experience supernatural love, joy, peace, and patience. They are interdependent, able to give and to receive. In general, these people are aware that God is in every conversation. He hears everything that they say. He knows their heart. They truly live in relationship with Him, praying without ceasing (in tune with Him), depending upon Him. Supernatural love and supernatural gifts can flow in this type of marriage or relationship. Are you overwhelmed yet? Of course, none of us is able to live this perfect life and relationship style. However, the more we grow in these attributes through healing, deliverance, and a disciplined, Spirit-led lifestyle, the healthier our relationships with God and others become.

On the next page, you will find a comparison of codependency and kingdom living. Study the chart, then complete this assignment:

INDIVIDUAL ASSIGNMENT #4a

After studying the chart on the next page, list below the people with whom you may have some codependency: those whose approval you desire, people to whom you have difficulty saying "no", people who always seem to get their way when interacting with you, people with whom you sense you may have some unfinished business or codependency. Think about how these relationships impact your marriage. Consider these same issues with your spouse if their behavior strongly affects your serenity. Place a star next to the principles in column two, Kingdom Living, that will help you to grow in these relationships.

1. Possible codependent relationships: _____

2. How do these relationships affect your marriage _____

3. What signs of codependency do you see in your marriage? _____

SESSION #4, pp. 73 - 82

CODEPENDENCY	KINGDOM LIVING: Luke 6:27ff
ISa.16:7 "...for the Lord seeth not as man seeth; for man looketh on the outward appearance (MASK), but the Lord looketh on the heart." It is a heart issue.	
Self Centered. What about **ME**? All fear is pride based. Pro.16:18 "Pride goeth before destruction, and an haughty spirit before a fall." We compare ourselves to others and determine that we are better or worse than them...both conclusions are prideful. IICo.10:12.	God-Centered. Whatever you desire, God. Jn.4:16a "And we have known and believed the love that God hath to us..." KNOW that God loves you. No need to gain it or prove worth.
React to people. Respond in kind. Immature. I can only "love" those who "love" me and fulfill my expectations. If someone has a "need", I must respond to it, even if it robs them of an opportunity to grow. Job6:22-23 "Did I say "Bring unto me? or, Give a reward for me of your substance? Or, Deliver me from the enemy's hand? Or, Redeem me from the hand of the mighty?" Job was not asking for help. He just wanted some support and love.	Respond to God. Mature. Selfless. Is.6:8 "...Then said I, Here am I; send me." ICo.12:23 To the less lovely, the more difficult to love, give more love. ❖ This is God's economy, to give what has not been earned, what does not seem deserved. ❖ This is supernatural love, beyond our natural ability.
Enemy's Plan: Jn.10:10 "The thief cometh not but for to steal, and to kill, and to destroy, I am come that they might have life, and that they might have it more abundantly.'	Jer. 29:11; Ro.8:28-29. Because our heart is turned toward God, even evil is used for our good. Crisis and difficulty is seen as an opportunity to grow. We are not compelled to "fix" everyone's problems, but we are able to support them as they also have an opportunity to grow through their pain.
Our identity and feelings are based upon another person or event. "I can't be happy unless you.... (are happy, treat me a certain way, compete a certain goal, etc.)" I'm sick of this job. I can't wait until vacation next week." This is not the normal anticipation of pleasure, but a pattern of escape that allows us not to live in the present. Another symptom is a lifestyle of instant gratification. He.13:5 "...Be content with such things as ye have..." • Victim responses: "I don't care." Or "I shall not be moved." • You must not fail, or I will be a failure. • Control / Rebellion / Rejection • Witchcraft prayers	Jn.3:16 "For God so loved the world that He gave His only begotten Son..." I am His bondservant Jesus was moved by compassion and so am I. Mt.9:36 "But when He saw the multitudes, He was moved with compassion on them..." But He also only did what He saw His Father do. Jn.8:29. No favorites respect and see potential in each person. Ja.3:17. See the end from the beginning. Is.46:10 "Declaring the end from the beginning..."
Lu.6:32 "For if ye love them which love you, what thank have ye? for sinners also love those that love them."	From Luke 6:27-28: Love your enemies. Pray for those who despitefully use you
Eros "love" does not feel like love to the receiver because it is self serving.	Agape: endless, steady, unconditional love. Jer.31:3 "...I have loved thee with an everlasting love..."
Words and actions are selected based upon a desired outcome. (Manipulation). I do what I want to do. Ro. 7	Do what the Father does. Jn.8:29 Say what the Father does. Jn.8:26 and 28.
Fishing (Hook) ...payoff. Even though I insist that I hate the habit, the behavior, or the unhealthy relationship, I cling to it because I am getting something out of it.	Life of grace and mercy, truth and righteousness. Ps.85:10. Receive the Father's love and give it away.

SESSION #4, pp. 73 - 82

STUDY GUIDE #4b
DISAGREEMENTS AND DIFFERENCES

According to Webster[13], a conflict is "a sharp disagreement or opposition (outward conflict); an emotional disturbance resulting from a clash of impulses in a person (inner conflict)." (parenthesis ours) When couples attempt to resolve disagreements or differences with one another before they resolve their personal feelings about the issue, they often enter into a conflict. One way to define conflict is to say that it is a negative emotional response to a difference affecting a relationship.

The phrase "unity with diversity" is a translation of "oneness" in Genesis 2:1-24. It implies that differences in marriage are inevitable but that they don't have to be a source of weakness. In fact, if couples learn to handle differences in a healthy way, they will become an opportunity for growth. If conflicts are avoided, the unresolved issue will probably arise at some point in the relationship and demand attention.

A humble attitude will help couples to resolve their differences quickly and with respect, regardless of the source of the conflict. The most significant fact about the conflicts a couple experiences is not how often they have them, but how regularly they resolve them. It is true, however, that a greater degree of healing often leads to less conflict and to conflicts that are more likely to result in growth. This is why we strongly encourage healing and deliverance ministry (Restoring the Foundations Ministry) for couples who are experiencing difficulties.

On the next pages, you will find a list of "Do's" and "Don'ts", guidelines for those who desire to grow as they face their differences. The "Do's" tend to shorten conflicts and make them more productive. The behaviors listed as "Don'ts" often prolong conflicts and make a healthy resolution unlikely. After a conflict, if each person involved will seek the Lord about the ways they prolonged it, they will receive insight into their patterns and they will be prepared to repent and to be changed.

AN EXPLANATION OF "TIME OUT"

One of the "Do's" that you will find on the list, is "Time Out". This concept requires a bit of explanation. At times, a couple will agree to take a "time out" during a conflict. This must always be by mutual agreement. Perhaps they need time to rest, to pray, or to pour out their hearts to the Lord for healing or direction. It is also possible that the conflict has come up at a time when there were other legitimate needs requiring their attention (care of a child, leaving for work or an appointment, etc.) Then the couple can take a "time out" as long as they first agree upon a specific time and place to continue their discussion. Some couples hesitate to do this because of the Scripture's admonition "not to let the sun go down on anger" Ep.4:26b. However, most couples find that the anger subsides as they come together and agree that they are committed to resolving the disagreement at a specific time. After a good night's sleep, conflicts are often simple to resolve! All that said, some couples prefer to stay up late in order to resolve a conflict, and, if it is productive, we don't discourage that.

---

[13] Webster's New World Dictionary, College Edition (United States of America: The World Publishing Company) 308

SESSION #4, pp. 73 - 82

DO'S

- GIVE UP YOUR "RIGHTS". Remember Jesus' example on the cross.
- USE THE FEELING FORMULA. Be honest about your feelings, but take them to the Lord and resolve them first.
- REMEMBER THAT YOU ARE TEACHING OTHERS HOW TO TREAT YOU.
- LISTEN PATIENTLY. Be just as interested in understanding the other person as you are in getting your own points across.
- GIVE GOOD FEEDBACK AFTER THE OTHER PERSON SHARES, BEFORE EXPRESSING YOUR OWN FEELINGS AND OPINIONS.
- STUBBORNLY REFUSE ALL THOUGHTS OF JUDGMENT.
  📖 **Finally, bretheren, whatsoever things are true, whatsoever things are honest, whatsoever things are just, whatsoever things are pure, whatsoever things are lovely, whatsoever things are of good report; if there be any virtue, and if there be any praise, think on these things." (Ph.4:8)**
- LOOK FOR CREATIVE SOLUTIONS. Can both needs/desires be met? Go to your second choice if both of you can agree on that.
- SOMETIMES AGREE TO DISAGREE when it is not crucial to the relationship. Give your partner the freedom to have a different opinion.
- TAKE A TIME OUT IF YOU NEED IT. Ask first. Set a goal to continue the conversation at a specific TIME and a specific PLACE and keep this commitment.
- AGREE ON SOMETHING. Coming into agreement on anything during a conflict tends to absolve anger and bring a constructive peace into the situation. Agree that you need to pray. Agree that a time out would help. Agree that you haven't followed good resolution skills. Agree on something.
- BE WILLING TO BE CHANGED. If each person will seek the Lord about the part they played in the conflict and the changes they need to make, resolution will begin.
- TRY BRAINSTORMING INSTEAD OF DISCUSSION, which can lead to conflict if the topic stirs a lot of feelings.
  - a) Set a time and a place to brainstorm.
  - b) During the intervening time, each person lists their ideas.
  - c) Get together and list all of the ideas on a large pad or board, alternating between the people involved, until all ideas are added. It is fine to add new ideas as the list sparks creativity. No comments are to be made as each idea is listed. No partiality is shown.
  - d) Take an open mind to each idea, not just your own.
  - e) Narrow the list down to those that seem like they may be acceptable to both of you.
  - f) Make your decision at this point, if you are ready.

SESSION #4, pp. 73 - 82

DON'TS

- DON'T BE CODEPENDENT. Focus on the changes YOU need to make, not on someone else's!

- DON'T BE STUBBORN. Remember that the point of conflict is often that the Lord wants to change you.

- DON'T BLAME. This is an attempt to avoid change by shifting focus and responsibility to the other person.

- DON'T TRY TO WIN. This means that the other person has to be a loser.

- DON'T BRING UP PAST HURTS YOU HAVE BEEN HOLDING ON TO. Acknowledge that the unresolved feelings are your responsibility and get them resolved.

- DON'T WITHDRAW. The unresolved issue will follow you around until you deal with it. You can't run away from it. Instead, if you need some space and time to pray, to think, and to resolve feelings, ask for a Time Out.

- DON'T BE A VICTIM. Victims never conquer. They feel sorry for themselves, but no one comes to their rescue.

- DON'T FOCUS MORE ON being understood than on being understanding.

INDIVIDUAL ASSIGNMENT #4b

1. In a conflict, which Don'ts (above) are you most likely to do? _____

2. In a disagreement, which feelings do you often experience? _____

3. Set three goals, based on the "Do's" on page 78 that you will prioritize? _____

4. Write out a brief description of a recent conflict. This will be used during your next joint session. _____

The Intimate Marriage (5)
© 2013 Paraklesis Ministries

SESSION #4, pp. 73 - 82

STUDY GUIDE #4c
AMENDS: WHEN REPENTANCE IS NOT ENOUGH

BE QUICK TO REPENT!
BE QUICK TO FORGIVE!
BE QUICK TO ALLOW THE LORD TO CHANGE YOU!

Husbands and wives who quickly forgive and repent live in the grace of God. As they extend grace to one another by forgiving, they are also likely to receive grace when they make a mistake and need to ask forgiveness. However, there is another step that couples need to take in order to assure growth if an offense is substantial or it becomes habitual. At that point, repentance will not restore the relationship. Amends will be required. Amends is giving 120%, in order to build and to restore. This is the "adding the fifth part thereto" referred to in Leviticus 5:16.

Like the amendments to the Constitution, the amends process makes allowances for adjustments in our character, habits, and personality. Amends incorporates the steps of forgiveness and repentance, but it adds the step of setting goals to make changes. For example, if one partner repents regularly for being late for church, but never talks about the steps they are taking to assure that they become victorious in this area, it is likely that the behavior will continue. At the very least, it is likely that the other partner will have difficulty trusting that their partner will change. Repentance is supposed to lead to change, but it is the process of amends that enables change. Making amends is substantially for the purpose of maturing the one who is asking forgiveness and making the changes. Making amends also builds trust in a relationship. It communicates that the person is truly repentant and does not intend to continue with the same behavior.

AMENDS: THE PROCESS OF CHANGE

1. ADMIT THE PROBLEM

📖 **"Search me, O God, and know my heart: try me, and know my thoughts: and see if there be any wicked way in me, and lead me in the way everlasting." (Ps.139:23-24)**
Let the Holy Spirit show you the attitudes and behaviors He wants to change.

2. FORGIVE OTHERS
    a. If you have ought against them: see Mk.11:25.
    b. If they have ought against you: see Mt.5:23

3. REPENT, saying "Will you please forgive me for …?" or "I was wrong to…"

📖 **"For God resisteth the proud, and giveth grace to the humble." (1Peter5:5b)**
Repent to God and to man. (unless it would harm the person or cause unnecessary hurt). Don't minimize what you have done or say things like "<u>If</u> I have hurt you …". Just simply state that you were wrong and that you desire forgiveness by saying "Will you please forgive me for _____?"

SESSION #4, pp. 73 - 82

4. **BE COMPASSIONATE.**
📖 "Now I rejoice, not that you were made sorry, but that you sorrowed to repentance …" (2Co.7:8a)
   Show genuine compassion for the other person.

5. **FORGIVE YOURSELF**

6. **ASK THE HOLY SPIRIT TO SHOW YOU THE CHANGES YOU NEED TO MAKE.**
   a. Set short term goals
   b. Set long term goals
   c. Communicate these goals to your partner

7. **STAY OPEN WITH AMENDS.** In other words, if you ask your partner's forgiveness, they may forgive you, but they may also want to tell you how they felt about what happened. Listen with compassion and give good feedback. Don't defend yourself. Be humble, continuing to ask forgiveness until they have finished sharing what they wanted to say. If you are able to do this, your repentance is sincere.

RESTORATION: BEYOND AMENDS
At times, couples have experienced a significant loss of trust in their relationship. In spite of heartfelt repentance, forgiveness, amends, and healing ministry, there is still a need for restoration of trust. The Scriptures (Le5:16) clearly show that the one who has committed the grievous offence must often go beyond the usual measures if the relationship is to be restored. Practically speaking, this means that the partner who has been wounded will communicate to their partner, in writing, what it will take in order to restore trust. This request may be very basic but it is extremely important, as it will be instrumental in restoring their relationship.

INDIVIDUAL ASSIGNMENT #4c

1. Ask the Holy Spirit if there is any pattern in your life for which you need to make amends to your spouse? (Tardiness, keeping commitments, or other habit that you have not broken.) _____
_____

2. Pray now. Ask the Lord's forgiveness.

3. With God's help, set a goal that will help you to break this pattern and to grow in this area. Record your goal here: _____
_____
_____

4. Set a time to share this (#3, above) with your spouse and to ask their forgiveness. _____

FOURTH JOINT SESSION, pp.83 - 84

FOURTH JOINT SESSION

OPEN IN PRAYER

Express to the Lord the desires of your heart for this time together.

#1. REVIEW your questionnaires, pages 9-10 for engaged couples, 11-12 for married couples.

    a Are there issues from your relationships in your family of origin that are affecting your current relationship? _____ Describe the patterns that existed. (e.g. controlling parent, abuse, lack of boundaries, family secrets, lack of ability to share certain feelings, etc.)

    b. Set two goals, based on the skills you have been learning, which will reinforce the growth you desire in these areas. Share these with your partner.

#2. TAKE TURNS SHARING how you could relate to the Codependency teaching (pages 73-75). List goals to grow in this area. _____

#3. DISCUSS AND RESOLVE the conflicts each of you listed (#4, page 79). Write out a summary of how you resolve it. (See page 81-82), Amends: The Process of Change). Most often, the Holy Spirit will show <u>both</u> partners how they have contributed to the conflict. Be sure to work on your <u>own</u> changes. See pages 78-79 for "Do's" and "Don'ts". Pray if you reach a difficult place, asking the Lord to help.

FOURTH JOINT SESSION, pp.83 - 84

#4. Take turns sharing with each other about whether or not there has been a serious loss of trust in your relationship? _____

If there has been a loss of trust, has it been resolved? _____

If it has not been resolved, do you need to seek counsel? _____

If your answer was "yes", set a goal: who will you contact? _____
_____ And when? _____

If you do not require counsel, communicate and set a goal that will help you to be restored as a couple. Write out what your partner will need to do in order to restore the trust. _____

#5. ASK your partner if there is something you can do this week that will be a blessing to them. Set a goal to accomplish it:

_____

#6. CLOSE IN PRAYER

SESSION FIVE, pp. 87-105

SESSION FIVE
Study Guide #5a: Husband and Wife 87
Study Guide #5b: Submission and Unity 95-97
Study Guide #5c: Breaking Habits (Optional) 99-105
INDIVIDUAL ASSIGNMENTS #5a,b,c and questions to answer . 89,91-94,98,101,104
JOINT SESSION #5 107

IF YOU ARE COMPLETING THIS AS A SELF HELP WORKBOOK:
1. Each person should complete all reading and answer all questions on pages 87-105. **Highlight or underline** significant points as you read. Please fill in every blank and answer all questions, as you will need these answers for your joint sessions.
2. Within 1-2 weeks, on the date you set for your joint session (see schedule on page 7), meet with your spouse/fiancée to complete together the Joint Session #5 on page 107.

IF YOU ARE RECEIVING MINISTRY:
1. Complete all reading and answer all questions on pages 87-105. **Highlight or underline** significant points as you read. Please fill in every blank and answer all questions, as you will need these answers for your ministry session.
2. When assigned, meet with your spouse/fiancée to complete together the Joint Session #5 on pages 107.

The Intimate Marriage (5)
© 2013 Paraklesis Ministries

SESSION FIVE, pp. 87-105

SESSION FIVE, pp. 87-105

STUDY GUIDE #5a
HUSBAND AND WIFE

MARRIAGE

Like the instruments in a beautiful symphony, a husband and wife bring diversity to their marriage. Over time, God blends the two into one harmonious display of His glory, a masterpiece of His creation, a sign to the earth of God's love for mankind.

Although God has ordained that marriages would demonstrate His glory, He has always known that this would not happen without the process of sanctification. He can use the marriage relationship to place pressure on us to grow in the areas where we do not conform to the image of His Son. Couples marry with love in mind, but it is their love for Jesus that makes them willing to be changed and able to have excellent marriage. Even couples with good relationships make mistakes and struggle through some of the seasons of their marriages, but if their problems are handled with wisdom, the results are extraordinary! Through trials and mountain top experiences, the Lord smoothens the rough places in their characters, and brings them into an intimate, harmonious relationship.

A couple that functions harmoniously is strong - able to accomplish their God-ordained purpose. Because they are able to resolve issues as they arise, they are not bogged down with the continual need for emergency maintenance. They have the grace, and the passion, to fulfill their destiny.

📖 **Likewise, ye husbands, dwell with them according to knowledge, giving honour unto the wife, as unto the weaker vessel, and being heirs together of the grace of life; that your prayers cannot be hindered." (IPt.3:7)**

Don Mears, pastor of Evangel Temple in Washington, D.C., says husbands and wives are "equal, but functionally different." Just as the uses and properties of a clay pot and a crystal vase are distinctive, the functions, qualities, strengths, and weaknesses of a husband and wife are unique and complimentary. In the Trinity, we clearly see that Jesus submitted fully to the Father. In fact, He gave His life for us in complete agreement with His Father's will. This in no way lessened his value or significance. In like manner, a husband and a wife are equal, although their roles are different.

A GODY HUSBAND IS A SERVANT LEADER (Ep.5:23)

Ecclesiastes 7:18 reads: "It is good that thou shouldest take hold of this; yea, also from this withdraw not thine hand: for he that feareth God shall come forth of them all." In this Scripture, we find the principle of holding two truths in tension. Often, there are two biblical principles that seem contradictory, but both are true. We are to "hold on" to both of them. With wisdom, we will be able to discern the appropriate truths that apply in each situation we encounter. The husband's title, servant leader, is one of these seeming contradictions. How is it possible to serve and, at the same time, to be a strong leader? However, as we study Jesus' example of leadership, the essence of the role becomes clearer. Jesus loved His bride to the point that He was willing to give up everything for her. He gave His life for her. And yet, this is the same God Who declared that the only way to the Father is through the Son. He said that no one could be saved without accepting Jesus as Lord and Savior. The pattern that Jesus set is both that of the supreme servant and the mighty leader.

The category of highest priority for the husband is in the area of his relationship with God. This foundational aspect of a man's life must be in order for the remainder of his role to be carried out properly.

A GODY WIFE IS HER HUSBAND'S COMPLETEMENT (Gn.2:18)

God is a God of order. For some, the concept of order implies restriction, but the hallmark of marriages in which there is unity and order, is a great sense of purpose and unity. God has ordained certain parameters in which husbands and wives are to function, and he has set the husband as head of the home and the wife as her husband's helpmeet, his completement. The Lord provides grace for a wife who is willing to submit to her husband with a respectful attitude. First, she should share her feelings and discernment with her husband. She should ask her husband to carefully consider and pray about what she has shared. At that point, she can release her opinion and come into agreement with her husband, doing all she can to bring the chosen course of action to pass. There is great freedom for people of all different personality types within this divine pattern, but there is a notable order. Even god subjected himself to these principles in the trinity. The three persons of the godhead are equal, and yet functionally different. Jesus also submitted himself to the will of the father as he laid down his life for his bride. This did not lessen his value or his worthiness. In fact, for his humility, his father gave him the name that is above every name ever named, Jesus! (ph.2:5-11) it is a great honor to be able to lay down our lives, our desires and our opinions for the love of another.

SESSION FIVE, pp. 87-105

INDIVIDUAL ASSIGNMENT #5a

1. On pages 91-92 you will find several Scriptures related to the roles of a husband. Beneath each Scripture, you will find a checklist of qualities. Please follow these instructions:

    a. Husband (or husband-to-be)

        i. Place an "S" next to the areas you consider your strengths.

        ii. Place a ✓ next to several areas where you see a need for personal growth.

    b. Wife (or wife-to-be)

        i. Place an "S" next to several areas you consider HIS strengths.

        ii. Place a ✓ next to 1 (ONE ONLY) area where you suggest a need for growth.

2. On pages 93-94 you will find several Scriptures related to the roles of a wife. Beneath each Scripture, you will find a checklist of qualities. Please follow these instructions:

    a. Wife (or wife-to-be)

        i. Place an "S" next to the areas you consider your strengths.

        ii. Place a ✓ next to several areas where you see a need for personal growth.

    b. Husband (or husband-to-be)

        i. Place an "S" next to several areas you consider HER strengths.

        ii. Place a ✓ next to 1 (ONE ONLY) area where you suggest a need for growth.

SESSION FIVE, pp. 87-105

SESSION FIVE, pp. 87-105

	ROLE OF THE HUSBAND
📖	"Be kindly affectioned one to another with brotherly love; in honour preferring one another." (Ro.12:10)
	☐ Has a servant's heart. (Mt.20:25-28) ☐ Lays down his life for his wife. Is willing to put her needs before his. ☐ Blesses his wife with his words of encouragement, edification and comfort, even in difficult times.
📖	"That he might sanctify and cleanse it with the washing of the water by the word."(Ep.5:26) (This is the Rhema word. What is God saying at this time?)
	☐ Reads the Bible with her, seeking to hear a present, applicable word from the Lord. ☐ Lives the Word. ☐ Bases decisions and actions on the current direction of the Holy Spirit. ☐ Encourages his wife in her walk with the Lord.
📖 "	So ought men to love their wives as their own bodies. He that loveth his wife loveth himself. For no man ever yet hated his own flesh; but nourisheth it and cherisheth it, even as the Lord the church" (Ep.5:28-29) (Note: To Cherish is to soften with warmth)[14]
	☐ Takes time to listen to and talk with his wife regularly. (Often, this is one of a wife's greatest blessings.) ☐ Shares vulnerably about his feelings and experiences. ☐ Is comfortable allowing his wife to share about her concerns and her difficulties. ☐ Gives good feedback, not taking responsibility to "solve" her feelings. (see p.30) ☐ Is physically and verbally affectionate. (Shows physical affection regularly, not just prior to sexual relations.) ☐ Has a habit if repentance, asks forgiveness and forgives easily.
📖	"For this reason a man will leave his father and his mother and be faithfully devoted to (shall be joined, KJV) to his wife, and the two shall be in one flesh". PNT[15] (Ep.5:31)
	☐ Promotes unity within his marriage. ☐ Keeps priority on relationship with God and then his wife…before all others.
📖	"But then you one by one, each must continually love his own wife just as himself" PNT[16] (Ep.5:33a)
	☐ Loves his wife all the days of his life. ☐ Never threatens divorce.

---

[14] Vine, Unger, white
[15] William J. Morford, <u>The Power New Testament, Revealing Jewish Roots</u>, A Translation of the 1993 Fourth Edition United Bible Society Greek Manuscript (Lakeland, Florida: William J. Morford, 1996) 262
[16] Morford

	ROLE OF THE HUSBAND, cont'd
📖	**"For I would have you know, that the head of every man is Christ (1Co.11:3a)**
	☐ Is submitted to God, yielded to Him. ☐ Takes time for regular prayer and Bible study. ☐ Is led by the Holy Spirit, desiring constant communion with Him. ☐ Understands and applies the principle of delegation.
📖	**"For the husband is head of his wife, even as Christ is the head of the church." (Ep.5:23a)**
	☐ Is a servant leader. ☐ Seeks God, with his wife, and writes out the vision. ☐ Clarifies and expands the vision on a regular basis. (Some couples do this at the beginning of each New Year) ☐ Prays with his wife on a regular basis. (Suggestions, pages 15-17) ☐ Is decisive when necessary.
📖	**"Likewise, ye husbands, dwell with them according to knowledge, giving honour unto the wife, as unto the weaker vessel, and being heirs together of the grace of life; that your prayers be not hindered." (1Pt.3:7)**
	☐ Relates to his wife with wisdom and an understanding of her unique personality. ☐ Shows respect for his wife. ☐ Values her opinions and requests her input. ☐ Provides security. (physical, emotional, spiritual)
📖	**"Submitting yourselves one to another in the fear of God." (Ep.5:21)**
	☐ Has a humble attitude. ☐ Carefully considers wife's discernment. ☐ Seeks confirmation and support for decisions.

SESSION FIVE, pp. 87-105

	ROLE OF THE WIFE
📖	"Wives, submit yourselves to your own husbands, as unto the Lord." (Ep.5:22)
	☐ Able to trust the Lord. ☐ Has a habit of time with the Lord: prayer, Scripture and desire for continual communion with the Holy Spirit. ☐ Trusts her husband, knowing that God works through him. ☐ Allows her husband to make mistakes and to learn from them. Knows that God can use them for good. ☐ Able to receive comfort from the Lord and from her husband. ☐ Communicates her needs and desires to her husband.
📖	"Whose adorning let it not be that outward adorning of plaiting the hair, and of wearing of gold, or of putting on of apparel; but let it be the hidden man of the heart, in that which is not corruptible, even the ornament of a meek and quiet spirit, which is in the sight of God of great price. For after this manner in the old time the holy women also, who trusted in God, adorned themselves, being in subjection unto their own husbands." (1Pt.3:3-5)
	☐ Is submitted to her husband ☐ Has a right attitude of heart ☐ Is an encouragement and a good example to other wives.
📖	"and the wife see that she reverence her husband."(Ep.5: 33b)
	☐ Respects her husband. ☐ Speaks highly of him in front of others, including children. ☐ Is able to come into unity with her husband, with a good attitude. ☐ Is physically receptive and affectionate. ☐ Has a habit of repentance. Asks forgiveness and forgives easily.
📖	"The heart of her husband doth safely trust in her" (Pr.31:11a)
	☐ Is trustworthy and faithful. ☐ Keeps her word.
📖	"She will do him good and not evil; all the days of her life." (Pr.31:12)
	☐ Her desire is to bless her husband. She seeks ways to do this creatively. ☐ Blesses her husband with words of encouragement and edification, even in difficult times. ☐ Never threatens divorce. ☐ Loves her husband all the days of her life.
📖	"She stretcheth out her hand to the poor; yea she reaches forth her hands to the needy." (Pr.31:20)
	☐ She has a heart to serve, first those at home, then others. ☐ She is committed to the vision for the marriage, desiring to be used by the Lord.
📖	"She maketh herself coverings of tapestry; her clothing is silk and purple." (Pr.31:22)
	☐ She maintains a feminine and attractive appearance.

SESSION FIVE, pp. 87-105

	ROLE OF A WIFE, cont'd
📖	**"Strength and honour are her clothing"** (Pr.31:25)
	☐ Inner virtues and character development are important to her. ☐ Is not given to a habit of worry.
📖	**"She openeth her mouth with wisdom; and in her tongue is the law of kindness." (Pr.31:26)**
	☐ Her tongue is disciplined; her words are edifying. ☐ Communicates openly and honestly.
📖	**"She looketh well to the ways of the household"** (Pr.31:27)
	☐ The home is neat and clean. (This will involve teamwork.) ☐ The atmosphere of the home promotes feelings of comfort, well being and welcome. ☐ Provides godly music and other reminders of the Lord in the home.

SESSION FIVE, pp. 87-105

STUDY GUIDE #5b
SUBMISSION AND UNITY

 "Submit yourselves therefore to God." (Ja.47a)
 "Submitting yourselves to one another in the fear of God." (Ep.5:21)
 "Wives, submit yourselves unto your own husbands, as unto the Lord." Ep.5:22

A word to husbands

Although God has placed you as the head of your home, He has not called you to dominate your wife. He has asked you to cherish her and to relate to her with wisdom and humility, to release her into her fullest potential. Be open about your discernment while expressing regard and respect for hers, as she is your completement. Be a servant leader. This builds respect, trust and unity. lay down your life and love your wife as Christ loved the Church. At times, the Holy Spirit will lead you to die to your own desires and opinions and come into agreement with your wife. At other times, He will show you that you need to stay strong with what He has given you at that point.

A word to wives

Your capacity to trust the Lord will increase as you develop your ability to work in unity with your husband. Relate to him with respect and meekness ("gentle, inner strength"). Be open about your discernment while showing regard and respect for his. This will enhance his leadership and your partnership with him. Avoid control and yield to God. There may be occasions when you are still not able to agree and a decision must be made. Then, except in areas of sin, if you will lay down your personal desires and wholeheartedly support the decision, the Lord will bring your heart into agreement with your husband's. Desire to understand his perspective, and then ask yourself "How can I help this come to pass?"

IDEALLY, HUSBANDS AND WIVES WILL CONTINUALLY GROW IN THEIR ABILITY TO FUNCTION AS A TEAM, TO BE CO-LABORERS WITH GOD, IN SUBMISSION TO AND LED BY THE HOLY SPIRIT.

 "Except a corn of wheat fall into the ground and die, it abideth alone: but if it die, it bringeth forth much fruit." (Jn.12:24) When you die to your own desires, there is a release of power in your life and in your marriage. Submission produces strength, not weakness.

SUBMISSION IS MAINLY AN ATTITUDE OF THE HEART

It is our heart that God is after. When a decision is made, provided that it is not sinful, the attitude we have toward Him and toward one another is ultimately more important to him than the decision we made.

SESSION FIVE, pp. 87-105

📖 "**Submitting yourselves one to another in the fear of God. Wives, submit yourselves to your own husbands, as unto the Lord. For the husband is head of his wife, even as Christ is the head of the church: and He is the saviour of the body. Therefore as the church is subject unto Christ, so let the wives be to their own husbands in every thing. Husbands, love your wives, even as Christ also loved the church and gave himself for it; that he might sanctify and cleanse it with the washing of the water by the word, that he might present it to himself a glorious church, not having spot, or wrinkle, or any such thing; but that it should be holy and without blemish. So ought men to love their wives as their own bodies. He that loveth his wife loveth himself. For no man ever yet hated his own flesh; but nourisheth it and cherisheth it, even as the Lord the church: for we are members of His body, of his flesh, and of his bones. For this cause shall a man leave his father and mother, and shall be joined unto his wife, and they two shall be one flesh. This is a great mystery: but I speak concerning Christ and the church. Nevertheless let each one of you in particular so love his wife even as himself; and the wife see that she reverence her husband.**" (Ep.5:21-33)

The concept of submission is often misunderstood, eliciting fear of control or other negative expectations. In truth, submission is an attitude of the heart and the Bible exhorts husbands and wives to submit to God, wives to submit to their husbands, and both husbands and wives to submit to one another. As couples seek to learn to work together, they become adept at discerning the will of God. After all, they are not seeking their own will, but rather, they are seeking to know what the Lord wants them to do. It is the will of God that automatically brings husbands and wives into unity on important issues if they are willing to wait on the timing of God.

IF A HUSBAND AND WIFE HAVE A DIFFERENCE OF OPINION:

1. Pray. Above all, desire to know God's will.
2. Share your discernment with each other.
3. Discuss options and concerns, agreements and differences. Value and carefully consider each other's perspectives and discernment.
4. Pray again, asking the Lord to bring you into unity with His will.
5. Avoid making significant decisions without unity. If you are not in agreement and a decision does not NEED to be made at this time, then delay the decision. If you are not in agreement and the decision DOES NEED to be made at this time, you will usually go with what the Husband is sensing, unless he believes he should come into agreement with what his wife is hearing.

UNITY WITH DIVERSITY

📖 "**Male and female created he them; and blessed them, and called their name Adam in the day when they were created.**" (Ge.:5:2)

SESSION FIVE, pp. 87-105

📖 **"and the two shall be in one flesh" PNT**[17] **(Ep.5:31)**
God considers and relates to a husband and wife as ONE. Think about the implications! There are many. For example, it is common for each spouse to "see" just a portion of their vision. As they communicate this information to one another, they begin to see more and more of the picture. Their perceptions are multiplied as they are shared, not just added together. This same principal applies to other instances when a couple desires or needs to hear from the Lord. Often, the greater the flow of unity between a husband and wife, the deeper and more intimate their communication with the Lord.

📖 **"For we are members of His body, of his flesh, and of his bones" (Ep. 5:30**
📖 **"This is a great mystery: but I speak concerning Christ and the church"**
Because God ordained that a man and his wife should reflect the love of Christ and the church, the Scriptures which refer to unity in the church lend much insight into God's plan for marriage. Two excellent references for these principles are the seventeenth chapter of John and the second chapter of Philippians.

📖 **" If there is any admonition in Messiah, if there is any consolation of love, if any fellowship of the Spirit, if any compassions and mercies, you must make my joy complete, so that you would cherish the same views, since you have this love, of one accord, thinking the same thing, and not according to a facetious spirit, and not according to conceit, but in humility esteeming one another more than yourselves, who are also in Messiah Jesus, Who was in the form of God, did not think equality with God was robbery, but He laid aside His own equality, taking the form of a servant, when He came in a likeness of a men: and, when He was found in a manner of life as a man, He humbled Himself, then He became obedient unto death, even of a death of the cross. On this account then God raised Him to the highest rank and He freely gave Him the name above every name, so that at the name of "Jesus!" every knee of the heavenlies and the earthly and those below the earth would bow and every tongue would confess that Jesus Messiah is Lord in the glory of God our Father." PNT   (Ph.2:1-11)**

📖 **"You are to shine like stars in the world, presenting as lights a message of life..." PNT   (Ph.2:15b, 16a)**
A husband and wife, like the strings of a violin, are designed to be in harmonious relationship ("unity with diversity"). The picture that is painted in the Scriptures which refer to the "accord" in marriage and in the church, is that of a "concert of instruments"[18], a beautiful symphony. It is this love, this harmony that reveals the light of Jesus and draws the world to Him. It is one of the greatest testimonies of the power and love of God in this dark and hurting world.

---

[17] William J. Morford, The Power New Testament, Revealing Jewish Roots, A Translation of the 1993 Fourth Edition United Bible Society Greek Manuscript (Lakeland, Florida: William J. Morford, 1996) 262
[18] James Strong, LL.D., S.T.D. The New Strong's Exhaustive Concordance of the Bible (Nashville, Camden, Kansas City: Thomas Nelson Publishers, 1984)

SESSION FIVE, pp. 87-105

INDIVIDUAL ASSIGNMENT #5b

1. What can you do in order to grow in your ability to come into unity in decision-making?

2. What did you learn about marriage and submission in this teaching?

SESSION FIVE, pp. 87-105

STUDY GUIDE #5c
BREAKING HABITS

- **"For if ye live after the flesh, ye shall die: but if ye through the Spirit do mortify the deeds of the body, ye shall live."** Ro.8:13

It is possible to learn to walk in His grace, led by His Spirit, free of the bondage of habits. He is our hope. He is our liberty.

- **"Stand fast therefore in the liberty wherewith Christ hath made us free, and be not entangled again with the yoke of bondage."** Ga.5:1

It is God's desire that we would be free of all habits that could become harmful or sinful. However, if we attempt to free ourselves by sheer willpower, we will only increase the entrapment.

- **"But if ye will not drive out the inhabitants of the land from before you; then it shall come to pass, that those which ye let remain of them shall be pricks in your eyes, and thorns in your sides, and shall vex you in the land wherein ye dwell."** Nu.33:55

- **"My heart panted, fearfulness afrighted me: the night of my pleasure hath he turned into fear unto me."** Nu.21:4

If we continue in these habits, there will come a time when what used to bring us pleasure will cause us pain. The purpose of the pain is to motivate us to cease the habit before it brings destruction to our lives and our relationships.

- **"He that walketh with wise men shall be wise: but a companion of fools shall be destroyed."** Pr.13:20

- **"Blessed is the man who walketh not in the counsel of the ungodly, nor standeth in the way of sinners, nor sitteth in the seat of the scornful."** Ps.1:1

If we associate with those who are struggling with the behavior that we are committed to avoid or to break, it is much more likely that they will have a negative influence upon us than it is that we will be able to help them break their habit. Jesus did minister to many who were entrapped in sin, but his closest friendships were with those who were fully committed to God.

On the other hand, support in a group of other Christians who are sincerely making the effort to break similar habits may be instrumental in our freedom from them. Home church meetings are also helpful because they provide accountability, prayer and support, all of which are essential to success.

- **"The light of the body is the eye: if therefore thine eye be single, thy whole body shall be full of light. But if thine eye be evil, they whole body shall be full of darkness. If therefore the light that is in thee be darkness, how great is that darkness!"** Mt.6:22-23

What we look upon enters the gate of the whole body and either strengthens or weakens our character. Habits involving the use of the eye are deceptively destructive.

SESSION FIVE, pp. 87-105

WHAT ARE ADDICTIONS OR SINFUL HABITS?

Some, like pornography, are immoral, and they are sinful for all people. Others are amoral. These may be sinful for some, but may not be for all. Almost any behavior that becomes obsessive and steals time from relationship with God or family must be considered to have become an occasion of sin.

You are responsible for knowing God's will for you in regard to the choices you make in each of these areas. Even if the possibility of future addiction is slim, isn't your commitment to God and your complete freedom to serve Him much more important? For this reason, we strongly encourage you to avoid or discontinue any behavior which could possibly stand in the way of your total commitment to God's service. Some people see how close they can come to sin without actually "crossing the line". Why not express your love for God by walking a path which is as far from sin as possible?

Place a check ☑ beside any behaviors on this list which you think the Lord may want you to change at some point in your life. At the appropriate time, He will give you the grace you need in each area.

Behaviors to consider: (some are addicting, some are sinful, some are life threatening, some commonly lead to divorce, others cause ongoing conflict and resentment)
- ☐ pornography
- ☐ other sexual sin (describe _____)
- ☐ money problems
- ☐ anger problems
- ☐ passive aggressiveness
- ☐ codependency
- ☐ gambling
- ☐ overeating
- ☐ under eating
- ☐ lying
- ☐ sneakiness
- ☐ procrastination
- ☐ TV or movies which portray violence or sinful behaviors
- ☐ smoking
- ☐ thrill seeking
- ☐ compulsions (even "innocent" habits like use of the computer, telephone, TV, reading, etc. can become excessive and cause problems for some).
- ☐ foul language
- ☐ habitual tardiness (this has caused considerable longstanding conflict in some relationships)
- ☐ Others _____
- ☐ drugs or other chemicals. Even prescriptions or over the counter medications can become habitual.
- ☐ use of alcohol[19] and/ or drinking and driving.

---

[19] Consult your doctor when discontinuing a substance that has been addictive.

SESSION FIVE, pp. 87-105

IF YOU USE ALCOHOL, PLEASE COMPLETE THIS QUESTIONNAIRE [20]

☐ yes	☐ no	1. Have you ever decided to stop drinking for a week or so, but lasted only a couple of days?
☐ yes	☐ no	2. Do you wish people would stop nagging you about your drinking?
☐ yes	☐ no	3. Have you ever switched from one kind of drink to another hoping that would keep you from getting drunk?
☐ yes	☐ no	4. Have you had a drink in the morning during the past year?
☐ yes	☐ no	5. Do you envy people who can drink without getting into trouble?
☐ yes	☐ no	6. Have you had problems connected with drinking during the past year?
☐ yes	☐ no	7. Has your drinking caused trouble at home?
☐ yes	☐ no	8. Do you ever try to get extra drinks at a party because you did not get enough to drink?
☐ yes	☐ no	9. Do you tell yourself you can stop drinking anytime you want, even though you keep getting drunk?
☐ yes	☐ no	10. Have you missed days at work because of your drinking?
☐ yes	☐ no	11. Do you have "blackouts"?
☐ yes	☐ no	12. Have you ever felt that your life would be better if you did drink?

WHAT ARE SOME OF THE CAUSES OF ADDICTIONS OR SINFUL HABITS?
If feelings or conflicts aren't resolved, there is a lack of intimacy and a person becomes more prone to these behaviors in an unsuccessful attempt to have their needs met. In

---

[20] If you answered "yes" to four or more questions, this may indicate a problem with alcohol. Further evaluation/ministry is recommended.

'The twelve questions above are from the pamphlet "Is AA for you?". They are reprinted with the permission of A.A. World Services, Inc. Permission to reprint the twelve questions does not mean that A.A. has reviewed or approved the contents of this publication, nor that A.A. agrees with the views expressed herein. A.A. is a program of recovery from alcoholism only - use of the twelve questions in connection with the programs and activities which are patterned after A.A., but which address other problems, or in any other non-A.A. context, does not imply otherwise.

SESSION FIVE, pp. 87-105

addition to other causes, unhealed past experiences or generational curses can also make someone more prone to these habits.

WHAT CAN BE DONE ABOUT ADDICTIONS AND SINFUL HABITS?

📖 **"Our help is in the name of the Lord."** IISa.22:4.
At times, **professional help is necessary**, but God's word does provide the answer. It is in calling upon His name that we are freed. At the end of this section, we will look at the practical ways a person can apply God's plan for freedom in these areas.

Applying the principles in this book will increase the intimacy in your marriage and lessen the temptation to become involved in sinful habits. These healthy relationship skills also make it more likely that those who are convicted to discontinue certain behaviors will be successful.

Some of the general principles related to stopping behaviors are:

* receiving healing from the root cause of the addiction
* applying healthy relationship skills in the areas of communication and conflict resolution
* admitting the need/desire to quit
* soliciting the support and prayer of others
* resisting temptation several times in a row. Urges usually only last 5-10 minutes, then they pass.
* seeking professional help when needed
* accountability to a pastor, home group leader, counselor and/or other Christians
* substituting a healthy behavior
* realizing that "I can't" is not a bad thing to say
* learning that "Jesus can" and becoming adept at turning to Him for grace at times of temptation

If your reason for quitting is "good", but not "God", you will be more likely to stumble. For example, if your primary motive is your love for the Lord and your desire to please Him, success is much more likely.

In the process of becoming free of addictions or other habits, we need to understand and apply the principles regarding the relationship of sin and the law. Many of us have been carefully taught that it is weak to say "I can't." Actually, the Lord is waiting for us to come to the place where we are willing to admit that "we can't" so that we will turn to Him and receive His help.

SESSION FIVE, pp. 87-105

When we are tempted[21], if we react by trying to be righteous by our own efforts, we may temporarily be able to suppress the impulse and refuse to act upon it. However, because we have only redirected and not eliminated the expression of the impulse, it will eventually vent in other unhealthy ways. The more we strive to suppress the desires by our own strength, the stronger the temptation, and the need to express it. "In proportion to the determination to obey the law, the law and our sinful nature combine to drive us into unmanageable compulsions." However, if we react to temptation by restful prayer, realizing the impossibility of keeping the law without God, He will give us the victory. If we do yield to the sin, humble repentance will bring more grace (the desire and the ability to do God's will) into that area of our lives.

A word to the wise …
The best way to be free of bad habits is to avoid sin and all behaviors that are known to become problematic for some. Most people who develop addictions or sinful habits initiate the behavior believing that they are in control and that they will not allow it to control them. Often, they are deceived, and they gradually fall prey to the same bondage that has overtaken so many others before them. People whose families have a history of addictive behaviors need to give special consideration to this warning because they may be more likely to become ensnared. (Ex.20:4-6).

If you are a leader in the church or if you would like to be a candidate for a leadership role in the future, your decisions about this issue will impact not only your opportunities for leadership but also the lives of those you lead. In the Old Testament times, some children were set apart for God in a special way. They were consecrated to His service and they lived their lives (or a portion of their lives) under the Nasserite vow (Is.5:11, 22). In addition to other requirements this included the avoidance of alcoholic beverages and anything which could compromise their commitment to God.

It is possible to choose to live a life that is totally committed to God and to shun anything that might interfere with that dedication.

📖 **"Jesus said unto him, Thou shalt love the Lord thy God with all thy heart, and with all thy soul, and with all thy mind."** Mt.22:37.

PLEASE ANSWER THE QUESTIONS ON THE NEXT PAGE ……

---

[21] The principles in this section have been gleaned from John L. Sanford, Why Some Christians Commit Adultery, (Tulsa, OK: Victory House, Inc. 1989)

SESSION FIVE, pp. 87-105

INDIVIDUAL ASSIGNMENT #5c

1. List any behavior(s) which you sense the Lord is saying you need to discontinue at this time in your life. _____

2. Ask your partner if there are any habits they would like you to consider and pray about. List their answer here: _____

3. Pray and then set a goal to begin to deal with each of the pertinent behaviors listed above: (How will you do it? When will you do it?) _____

4. Ask the Holy Spirit to show you some of the root causes of the addiction or habit: (e.g. rejection, abandonment, fear of intimacy, lack of trust) _____

5. Ask the Lord to show some needs which you have been trying to meet by substituting these habits. (e.g. comfort, relaxation, relief from loneliness) List here: _____

6. Keeping your answer to question #4 in mind, ask the Lord what healthy behavior you can establish to replace the habit you are going to break: (for example, some people who quit smoking gradually begin an exercise program.) _____

7. Please study the four key habit breaking principles on the next page.

SESSION FIVE, pp. 87-105

SPIRITUAL KEYS TO VICTORY OVER HABITS

1. Realization that our own strength is never adequate.

2. A continual habit of repentance, which brings grace.

3. Patience. Don't ever give up on God. Sometimes the Lord gives us victory over habits suddenly. At other times, He deals with us gradually, but He always equips us to do all that He requires of us. Habitually require your flesh to cooperate with the grace of God.

4. Trust in the mercy and the power of God, Who is able to give us the victory.

SESSION FIVE, pp. 87-105

FIFTH JOINT SESSION, pp. 108

FIFTH JOINT SESSION

OPEN IN PRAYER

1. **TAKE TURNS** sharing with each other 4-5 of the strengths that you noted in your partner as you completed the assignment on pages 91-94.

2. **WIFE OR FIANCÉE:** share with your husband/fiancée the ONE (ONLY ONE) area in which you noted (on pp. 91-92) a potential area of need for them.

3. **HUSBAND/FIANCÉE**, receive this input graciously. Even if you can't relate to it at first, pray that God will help you to see their view point and to set goals for growth.

4. **HUSBAND OR FIANCÉE**, share with your wife/fiancée, the ONE (ONLY ONE) area in which you noted (on pp. 93-94) a potential area of need for them.

5. **WIFE/FIANCÉE**, receive this input graciously. Even if you can't relate to it at first, pray that God will help you to see their view point and to set goals for growth.

6. **BRAINSTORM** 5-10 things you could realistically enjoy together. (Going for a walk, a picnic, games with the children, holding hands, listening to music, reading side by side, going to the park, a quiet dinner after the children are in bed, going out for a cup of coffee or dessert, a weekend away, going to the library, travel, renting a movie, reading a book to one another, etc. etc.). Carefully follow the brainstorming instructions on page 78 and list your ideas here:

7. **DISCUSS** ways in which your marriage can be seen as an encouragement to others. Consider your manners, they way you speak about each other to friends, etc.

8. **PRAY OVER EACH OTHER.**

9. **CLOSE**

SESSION SIX, pp. 111-137

SESSION SIX
Vision and Five Year Plan 113
Budget 115
Sexuality 127
INDIVIDUAL ASSIGNMENTS #6a,b and questions to answer 117, 130
MASTERS FOR FORMS 113-114, 117, 119, 121
SIXTH JOINT SESSION 135-137

IF YOU ARE COMPLETING THIS AS A SELF HELP WORKBOOK:
1. Each person should complete all reading and answer all questions on pages 111-133. **Highlight or underline** significant points as you read. Please fill in every blank and answer all questions, as you will need these answers for your joint sessions.
2. Within 1-2 weeks, on the date you set for your joint session (see schedule on page 7), meet with your spouse/fiancée to complete together the Joint Session #6 on pages 135-137.

IF YOU ARE RECEIVING MINISTRY:
1. Complete all reading and answer all questions on pages 111-133. Highlight or underline significant points as you read. Please fill in every blank and answer all questions, as you will need these answers for your ministry session.
2. When assigned, meet with your spouse/fiancée to complete together the Joint Session #6 on pages 135-137

The Intimate Marriage (5)
© 2013 Paraklesis Ministries

SESSION SIX, pp. 111-137

SESSION SIX, pp. 111-137

STUDY GUIDE #6a
VISION AND FIVE YEAR PLAN

DO YOU KNOW WHERE YOU ARE GOING?

    📖 "Without a vision, the people perish." Pr.29:18.

    📖 "Write the vision and make it plain." Ha.2:2.

Often, we hear these Scriptures in regard to the vision for a church, but they are no less applicable to the vision for a marriage. A couple who has worked to develop good relationship skills will enjoy their marriage, but they will also be better prepared to fulfill the purpose for which the Lord has brought them together. One of the greatest joys of married life is for a couple to identify their God-given vision and to co-labor with the Lord to fulfill this plan.

Some people hesitate to write out their vision because they think it will constrain them. Others are not aware of the importance or the benefits of having a written vision. This exercise gives couples an opportunity to communicate and to come into agreement about their vision. It also gives them direction and a frame of reference that they can use when making decisions. Written visions are living documents, meant to be reviewed and revised over the years as additional insights, revelation, and knowledge are gained. We recommend that people review their written vision at the beginning of each year and revise it as necessary. It is also helpful to review the vision at times of significant decisions. The Lord often reveals His plan step by step, bringing clarity to issues addressed in the vision as the need arises.

A PERSONAL VISION

WILL ALWAYS COMPLIMENT AND SUPPORT

THE VISION OF THE MINISTRY/CHURCH

TO WHICH GOD HAS CALLED A COUPLE.

SESSION SIX, pp. 111-137

INDIVIDUAL ASSIGNMENTS #6a and b
PREPARING YOUR FIVE YEAR PLAN

EACH PARTNER SHOULD PREPARE A PLAN AND THEN, DURING THE JOINT SESSION, THESE PLANS WILL BE REVISED AND MERGED.

1. Seek the Lord in prayer then, on a separate piece of paper, write your preliminary vision.

2. Remember that it is not usually wise to undertake significant new responsibilities the first year of marriage.

3. We suggest that you refer to this plan and revise it as needed. Some couples pray together about this at the beginning of each year.

4. It may be helpful to review your personal prophecies for references to your gifts and callings.

5. Please add your final version of the plan to pp.113-114 during your joint session (page 135).

PLEASE INCLUDE:

1. A concise statement of your vision (also called a mission statement), with a Scripture reference. The statement may also be a specific Scripture.

2. Your prayer life, personal and as a couple.

3. Attendance at church activities (services, home care groups, marriage weekends, retreats, outreach opportunities, etc.)

4. Plans for further education and training.

5. Employment plans. (Include retirement plans if appropriate.)

6. Plans for children.

7. Do you plan to purchase a home or make other major expenditures?

8. Ministry opportunities (personal and plans as a couple).

9. Exercise and health needs. Life and health insurance. Will preparation and revision.

10. Make a copy of page 117. Use it to prepare next month's budget. (If you already have a successful budgeting process, you are welcome to use this form or, if you prefer, you may use your own form for your budget. Include health care provision, car maintenance costs, pocket money, savings for retirement and education, plans to eliminate debt, etc.

11. How will you do your budget? Who will pay the bills? Will you use credit?

12. List 5-10 joint activities that you both enjoy. Refer to your list on page 107. How often will you arrange a "date" or spend quality, planned time together?

13. List several activities of personal interest that each individual plans to pursue.

14. Review Prophecies for words that are relevant to your plan.

15. Ask the Holy Spirit if there is anything else He wants you to include.

SESSION SIX, pp. 111-137

Name(s) _____

Date _____

FIVE YEAR PLAN

Mission Statement: _____
_____
_____

SESSION SIX, pp. 111-137

Five Year Plan, cont'd

SESSION SIX, pp. 111-137

STUDY GUIDE #6b
BUDGET / FINANCIAL PLAN

📖 "For where your treasure is, there will your heart be also." (Mt.6:21)

If our desire is to serve the Lord in all we do, then our checkbook will reflect what is really important to us.

📖 "Bring ye all the tithes into the storehouse, that there may be meat in mine house, and prove me now herewith, saith the Lord of hosts, if I will not open you the windows of heaven, and pour you out a blessing, that there shall not be room enough to receive it. And I will rebuke the devourer for your sakes, and He shall not destroy the fruits of your ground…" (Ma.3:10-11)

As we bring in our tithe (10% of our gross income), the needs of the house of the Lord are met, and the Lord prospers us and protects us from the enemy. There may be seasons when our faith is tested. We may be tempted to withhold the tithe when times are tight. We may begin to believe the circumstances instead of the word of the Lord … to wonder <u>when</u> our finances will be blessed! But God is faithful. He keeps His word. In due time, as we persevere and allow Him to build our faith, He will prosper us.

📖 "He that hath a bountiful eye shall be blessed; for he giveth of his bread to the poor." (Pr.22:9)

After we have paid our tithe, we can seek the Lord about other opportunities to give into His work. It is easy to become so focused on our own financial needs that we don't respond to the prompting of the Holy Spirit to give to the needs of others. Know the joy of supporting those in need or contributing to those of like vision as the Lord puts them on your heart. Later, as your own vision is established or continues to develop, the Lord will place your needs on the hearts of others!

📖 "The rich ruleth over the poor and the borrower is servant to the lender."

1. Avoid debt.

2. If you are in debt, get out of debt.

If you follow these two recommendations, you will be completely free to serve the Lord with the finances He gives you, not obligated to any lender.

Assuming a loan for which you have collateral, such as a car or home loan, and making timely payments is not usually considered debt in the sense that we are discussing here. Often, these are wise investments. However, paying cash or paying off these loans as quickly as possible, is also advised.

SESSION SIX, pp. 111-137

If the Lord leads, consider giving rather than lending to those in need. If you lend, you bear an ongoing responsibility that you might prefer to avoid. You may chose to allow others to repay as they see fit rather than setting up a long term pay back.

Something to think about …

1. Take advantage of the strengths each of you have as you do your budget.

2. As you develop or update your budget, use the healthy communication skills you have been practicing. Maintain a respectful, cooperative attitude. You are a good team!

3. Some people fear that having a budget will cause them to feel trapped. Others avoid budgeting "because they don't have enough income". Nothing could be further from the truth. A budget brings peace of mind. It causes us to be able to enjoy the money we do spend because we know it is within our means. It quickly reveals problems (not enough income or too many expenses) which can then be resolved before they reach disastrous proportions. As you develop your budget and learn to use it, don't be discouraged if it takes you a while to work out a successful plan.

4. We suggest that engaged couples develop a potential budget, using their anticipated income and expenses. They could also take a shopping trip to price food and supplies for a typical month and to begin to learn to shop together.

5. If you aren't able to stay within your budget, it may mean that the budget is not realistic, or it could be that you need to increase your income and/or decrease your expenses, whichever option(s) you are able to accomplish. Budgeting problems must be identified and dealt with. They don't just "go away".

6. Maturity in this area brings great blessings to a marriage and to the kingdom of God, which prospers as we prosper!

📖 **"Well done, thou good and faithful servant: thou hast been faithful over a few things, I will make thee ruler over many things: enter into the joy of thy Lord."** (Mt.25:21)

God desires that we use all He provides for us, including our talents and finances, for His purpose.

SESSION SIX, pp. 111-137

BUDGET* FOR THE MONTH OF _____ **(PAYDAY** _____ **)**
(Master Form)

"A" STANDARD COSTS [40]	"B" FLUCTUATING COSTS" *
_____ Entertainment	_____ Tithe
_____ Groceries	_____ Offerings, Pledges
_____ Haircut	_____ Donations, Missions
_____ House or Rent	_____ Car maintenance
_____ Insurance	_____ Gas & Electric
_____ Auto	_____ Gifts
_____ Health	_____ Home Maintenance
_____ Homeowner's or renter's	_____ Licenses
_____ Life	_____ Cars
_____ Investment	_____ Drivers
_____ Loan or other debt	_____ Medical
_____ Newspaper	_____ Dentist
_____ Pocket Money	_____ Doctor
_____ Property Taxes	_____ Prescription
_____ Subscription	_____ Phone
_____ Tuition	_____ Vacation
_____	_____ Water
	_____ Miscellaneous
_____ "A" TOTAL STANDARD COSTS	_____ "B" TOTAL COSTS

BILLS	INCOME	NET
_____ "A"	_____	_____ "D"
+ _____ "B"	+ _____	- _____ "C"
_____ "C" TOTAL BILLS	_____ "D" TOTAL INCOME	_____ SAVINGS

Status of any current debt: **Current Totals: Savings / Investments**

_____ _____ _____   _____ _____

NOTES:
- Make copies of page 117 to use as a master monthly budget form and 119 for the annual periodic expenses.
- Include periodic costs (next page) that will occur during this budgeting period.
- Some periodic costs will be listed in the "Standard" column as they are always the same amount. Other periodic costs fluctuate and should be in the second column.
- If the budget is tight, you may need to project cash flow, using the form on page 121.
- Refer to page 123-125 for help with cash flow budgeting and specific financial needs.

Budget Review: At the end of the month, on separate paper, list areas of previous budget which were over or under forecast. Resolve any apparent budget problems.

---

[40] Standard costs remain the same monthly.

SESSION SIX, pp. 111-137

SESSION SIX, pp. 111-137

Yearly Periodic Expenses Master Form

(Keep a current record of these expenses, which are not paid every month. Revise this chart yearly and update it as changes occur (e.g. insurance premium is raised). Add the appropriate expenses to your copy of p.117 each month).

	Drivers licenses	Gifts	Insurance Health Life	Insurance Car Home	License Plates	Sub-scriptions	Taxes	Trips	Water
JAN									
FEB									
MAR									
APR									
MAY									
JUNE									
JULY									
AUG									
SEPT									
OCT									
NOV									
DEC									

The Intimate Marriage (5)
© 2013 Paraklesis Ministries

SESSION SIX, pp. 111-137

SESSION SIX, pp. 111-137

CASH FLOW BUDGET MASTER FORM

Month _____   **Starting   Balance**

Date	Income due: + amount	Date	Bill due: - amount	Balance

SESSION SIX, pp. 111-137

SESSION SIX, pp. 111-137

MISCELLANEOUS FINANCIAL PRINCIPLES

Although it can be difficult to look at a budget when finances are tight, it is imperative to face the situation and to prayerfully make decisions about how to handle it.

MONEY IN YOUR POCKET

When couples are not living by a budget, they sometimes fail to realize that having money in one's pocket is not the same as having money to spend. Before a dollar in the pocket is spent on anything you want, it is necessary to consider any payments that are due and any needs that haven't been met, as well as any liability that may have accrued. (i.e. Bills which are accumulating, even though they aren't due to be paid yet.) Even couples who have a surplus at times (income exceeds expenses) need to realize that they will have to put aside a certain amount each pay period so that when their periodic expenses (i.e. those which are not due each month, such as car insurance or taxes) come due, they will have sufficient funds to cover them.

SPENDING MONEY

We strongly encourage couples to budget a certain amount of spending money for each person. This is cash that you are free to spend or save for your personal use as you see fit. Even if this is a necessarily small amount, couples really seem to appreciate having it in the budget. We find that it increases the likelihood of faithfulness with other budget constraints. For the same reason, as well as for the health of your marriage, we advise the inclusion of a budget for regular "date nights" and/or family nights. This may be something as simple as walking to the dairy store for an ice cream cone or renting a DVD and making popcorn, but it is a special time set aside to "play" and to enjoy one another's company.

DEBT ELIMINATION. DON'T SPEND "TOMORROW'S MONEY TODAY"

When necessary, it is important to develop a plan for debt elimination because unnecessary credit places a strain on the marriage and the family. Debt causes people to spend "tomorrow's money today", so that when tomorrow comes, a significant portion of that money has already been spent, the debt must be paid, and couples are forced to live below their income level.

Prayerfully consider the following points regarding debt elimination:
- It is not likely that couples will get out of debt in the foreseeable future if they are only making minimum payments on their debts. They will need to do something to enable them to make larger payments on at least one of the debts.
- We do not advise couples to eliminate their tithe.
- If you are paying off any high interest loans, and you are unable to refinance them at a more reasonable rate, give priority to eliminating these debts. This may mean that you will make minimum payments on other loans temporarily and apply as much as possible to the high rate loan. If there are not any unusually high interest loans, we advise that you:
- Pay off the smallest debt first, then apply that monthly payment to the next smallest loan. For example, if there are five debts, we might suggest that you pay a certain amount on each bill per month (at least the minimum payment, so that you will not

- be assessed additional penalties). For example, let's assume that you are paying $25 a month on each of the five loans: When the smallest loan is paid in full, then you would take that $25 and add it to the payment on debt #2, so that you would be paying $50 a month on that second smallest debt. When the second smallest debt is paid in full, you would take that $50 and add it to the $25 you were paying on debt three, so that you would be paying $75 a month on debt three. And so on, until you are debt free. This method of payment enables you to retire debts systematically and it is an encouragement to see the progress. (e.g. "Now, we only have four debts, now we only have three debts, etc.)
- We would rather see slow, steady progress on debt reduction than to see a couple set unrealistic goals that they are not able to meet.
- Although we consider it acceptable to have a mortgage, and at times, a car loan, these payments must be reasonable and paid on time. If they are not, you may need to reassess your situation and make some changes.
- Most cities and many churches have consumer services for people who need help with their budgets.
- It is often possible for couples to avoid bankruptcy, even when the debts are considerable. Each debtor needs to be contacted to work out the terms of repayment. Many companies are willing to work with people who intend to pay off their debts rather than to claim bankruptcy because this is to their advantage.

BUDGET RECONCILIATION

Initially, it is important to reconcile the budget each month, in order to evaluate it's effectiveness and your compliance. To reconcile is to compare actual expenses and income items (line by line) with the budgeted amounts. (For example, we budgeted $100 for groceries, and we spent $92. We were $8 favorable to budget.)
- Budgeted expenses which were less than or the same as the amount planned are considered "favorable" to budget. (For example, we budgeted $50 for the phone bill, and it was $48, $2 favorable to budget.)
- Budgeted income which is more than or the same as the amount planned is considered "favorable" to budget. (For example, we budgeted $395 for my paycheck and I worked overtime and earned $425).

If overall, your performance is not favorable to budget (i.e. expenses were higher than budgeted and/or income was lower than budgeted), a couple will need to decide why it was unfavorable and make any necessary changes.
- Did you make unwise decisions?
- Did you receive the income you budgeted?
- Did you spend more than you budgeted?
- Was the budget realistic?
- Were there unexpected, but unavoidable expenses? If so, had you saved money in anticipation of these types of expenses?

The purpose of budget reconciliation is to determine problem areas in which you need to improve of your performance, and/or areas in which the budget needs to be revised so

SESSION SIX, pp. 111-137

that it more closely reflects a realistic picture of your needs. Couples are sometimes fearful that when they evaluate their performance (reconcile their budget) that it will show that they have not done well. It is very important to look at this as a learning process. It takes time to develop a good budget and to learn to live by it. If your performance is "unfavorable to budget", this does not always indicate a problem with you! It may be that the budget figures you are using are not adequate and that they need to be revised. Over the months, as you study your performance, you will be able to budget realistically and have confidence in your ability to project your needs. However, no matter how good a budget becomes, it must always be flexible (assume and prepare for unexpected costs) because it is not possible to anticipate every need which will arise.

Overall, many couples who resist the budgeting process due to the fear that it will restrict them, find that the opposite is true. Living by a budget brings great freedom. It is a pleasure to be free of worry and guilt and to know that you can truly enjoy the financial blessings the Lord provides, spending them according to the plan you and your partner have agreed upon.

CASH FLOW BUDGETING
In this method of budgeting, you will not only plan for the amounts of each expense and income item, they will also project the timing of each of them. Without this additional planning, if cash is quite tight, it is possible for a couple to pay their bills at the wrong time and to run into budget problems even if their income is adequate to meet their needs.

RECURRING FINANCIAL PROBLEMS may signal a lack of information and a need for instruction. However, like problems with a couples' sexual relationship, they may also point to a root issue, such as unresolved hurts or ungodly attitudes that require specific ministry. Ask the Holy Spirit to reveal root issues and to show you what ministry is needed. Because of the potential for devastation in a marriage, we advise couples to consult with a specialist, if necessary, for advice regarding persistent problems in the area of finances.

IF YOU NEED ADDITIONAL INFORMATION, we recommend Crown Ministry at www.crown.org.

SESSION SIX, pp. 111-137

SESSION SIX, pp. 111-137

STUDY GUIDE #6c
SEXUALITY IN MARRIAGE

(Engaged couples should study and pray as necessary in the areas of Soul Ties pp.131-132 and Love and Purity 133. More in depth exploration of the topic of sexuality should be covered just prior to the wedding.)

Recommended reading:
For married couples or for engaged couples to read individually shortly before the wedding:
Intended for Pleasure, by Ed and Gaye Wheat

Sexuality is often the topic of TV talk shows and magazine cover stories. But it is the Bible that presents God's plan for this aspect of a couple's relationship.

Sexuality is a gift from God and a blessing in a healthy marriage. However, some couples have underlying personal or relationship issues that are manifested as problems in their physical relationship. Other couples experience problems in this area because they are lacking information and insight. Generally speaking, a woman's attitude toward the physical relationship is strongly influenced by the level of intimate communication in the marriage. And a man who is denied sexual relations without due cause often feels very much like the woman who is denied intimate conversation. (Based upon Christopher Johnson's book "The Power That Women Have").

📖 **"Nevertheless, to avoid fornication, let every man have his own wife, and let every woman have her own husband. Let the husband render unto the wife due benevolence: and likewise also the wife unto the husband. The wife hath not power of her own body, but the husband: and likewise also the husband hath not power of his own body, but the wife. Defraud ye not one another, except it be with consent for a time, that ye may give yourselves to fasting and prayer; and come together again that Satan tempt you not for your incontinency." (1Co.7:2-5)**
A husband and wife fulfill a need for one another that, according to God's plan, cannot be met by anyone else. It is a serious matter to refuse physical relationship without good cause and mutual agreement. Although God's word says that a husband and wife have authority over each other's bodies, it also says that they are to treat each other with "due benevolence", or kindness. So, out of love and respect, a couple considers each other's needs and desires.

SESSION SIX, pp. 111-137

📖 **"Let thy fountain be blessed: and rejoice with the wife of thy youth. Let her be as the loving hind and pleasant roe; let her breasts satisfy thee at all times; and be thou ravished always with her love."** **(Pr.5:18-19)**

The fountain[41] referred to in this Scripture is the source of life, and the fountain from which children issue. It indicates that there is a spiritual and a natural blessing upon the marriage and the children of a marriage in which the husband and wife have a loving, committed and healthy sexual relationship.

A husband who is "ravished[42] always" with the love of his wife is captivated by her. He is inwardly delighted in her. i.e. he thinks thoughts about her which increase his love for her. (Ro.12:2) A wife who realizes that she is a delight to her husband is aware God's perspective on their relationship. Even couples who deal with the heartache of infertility can be fruitful as they impact others by fulfilling God's powerful call upon their lives.

📖 **"And when Boaz had eaten and drunk, and his heart was merry, he went to lie down at the end of the heap of corn: and she came softly, and uncovered his feet and laid her down."** (Ru.3:7)

Although this Scripture does not refer to the marriage relationship of Ruth and Boaz, we've placed it here as a reminder that we strongly encourage husbands and wives to go to bed at the same time when at all possible. This habit promotes a healthy physical relationship, but it also provides opportunities to hold one another and to share intimate conversation. During the seasons of life when you have a lot of responsibility, you may need to rely upon teamwork in order to be ready together, but this special time of day is well worth the effort it requires.

📖 **"But I am saying to you that everyone who looks at a woman with desire for her has already committed adultery with her in his heart."** PNT (Mt. 5.:28)

Adultery does not begin with a sexual relationship. It begins with casual looks, intimate conversations, and thoughts and comments about the attractiveness of someone other than your own spouse. It is never excusable, but it is more common in spouses who do not establish an intimate, heart to heart contact with their mate or spouses who have unhealed wounds from the past. You have been equipped through this course to cooperate with the Lord as He leads you into a more and more intimate relationship with Him and with each other. But don't ever hesitate to seek counsel if you need support. The success of your marriage and the fulfillment of your vision are deserving of all that you will need to invest.

We strongly advise couples to seek Christian counsel rather than to discuss questions and confidential details with their peers. The cause of difficulty in the sexual aspect of a couple's relationship can be as simple as a lack of basic knowledge. But it may also be due to other more complex problems. Regardless of the cause, if these problems are not resolved satisfactorily, they can lead to other destructive patterns in the marriage.

---

[41] **Vine, Unger, and White**
[42] **Vine, Unger and White**

SESSION SIX, pp. 111-137

Husbands and wives who feel unfulfilled or unsatisfied with their sexual relationship are often dealing with some other basic issue that needs to be resolved.

Some of the underlying causes of problems in a couple's sexual relationship include previous sexual abuse, soul ties to previous sexual partners, an ungodly soul tie between spouses, communication problems, inadequate conflict resolution, physical abnormalities requiring medical attention (e.g. these may cause painful intercourse or impotence), financial problems, lack of order or improper roles in the relationship, or a simple lack of knowledge. Depending upon the cause of a couple's problems, they may be able to work through them, or they may need to the help of a minister or counselor. Let's look at several possible causes of sexual difficulties and address some remedies for each:

previous sexual abuse: Requires specific ministry by a skilled minister/counselor. A person with a history of abuse may or may not be ready to face this issue at a particular time. If you know of or suspect this root problem, recommend supplementary ministry.

ungodly soul ties: The ministry guidelines and prayer for breaking ungodly soul ties is on 131-132. Soul tie ministry is necessary for counselees who have had any illicit sexual relationship prior to or during their marriage. This includes adultery and fornication. It is also indicated for couples who have had a premarital sexual relationship. Keep in mind that God intends that there would be a godly soul tie between marriage partners. Soul tie ministry is prayer to break ungodly soul ties. We also believe that an ungodly soul tie can form between parent and child when control is involved. This issue can interfere with the leaving and cleaving process, causing one partner to give less priority to their spouse's needs and desires than they do to their parent's.

premarital sexual relationship with their spouse: If this has occurred, study and then pray through the prayer on 131-132.

communication problems or inadequate conflict resolution: Because the sexual relationship is one way in which couples express (communicate) their love for one another, their abilities in the basic relationship skills (sharing and resolving feelings and conflicts) can enhance or detract from their sexual relationship. A husband and wife who are not accustomed to intimate conversation may not be very intimate in their sexual relationship either. Couples with unresolved hurts or resentments will probably have difficulty achieving a satisfactory sexual relationship also. By reviewing the instruction in sharing and resolving feelings as well as conflict resolution techniques and by giving couples an opportunity for additional practice of these principles, couples are sometimes able to have an intimate, fulfilling sexual relationship.

physical conditions requiring medical attention (e.g. these may cause painful intercourse or impotence): Please see page 80a for additional information. Impotence and other sexual dysfunction can also be caused by underlying physical problems that require medical attention. Suggest that couples consider this possibility when they are making a decision about how to handle sexual problems in their marriage.

financial problems, job loss: The pressures of unresolved financial problems or job loss can interfere with sexual appetites and function. As with underlying communication problems, ministry that resolves the underlying problem will sometimes resolve the sexual difficulty also.

lack of order or improper roles in the relationship: Husbands who feel disrespected and wives who do not feel cherished may not have much desire for a sexual relationship. Again, ministry to the underlying hurts, and instruction in the biblical concepts of the role of a husband and wife may resolve this problem.

lack of knowledge: Although the topic of sexuality is commonly discussed, the godly perspective is not often given. At times, couples have adopted unhealthy attitudes about their sexuality from their parents or poorly informed peers. Sometimes, counselees have been shamed (rather than wisely disciplined and informed) about an experience in childhood and they may have carried that shame into their marriage relationship. This is an indication of a need for healing. Even married couples often appreciate a frank discussion of the sexual act and an opportunity to have their questions answered. Couples who are engaged and some married couples prefer to ask their questions during their individual time with their counselor. Discuss basic information and attitudes with them. (See Session Six in the Biblical Marriage and Premarriage Ministry Manual). Encourage them to read a Christian book on sexuality (see the bibliography and the recommended reading list in this course). Also present these points:

- It is important to hug and to kiss at times other than when initiating a sexual relationship.

- The attitudes expressed and words spoken during the day have a significant effect upon a person's desire for sexual relations.

- Encourage couples to view sexual intimacy as an opportunity to express love to their partner and to meet their physical needs in a manner which satisfies deep emotional needs also.

In summary, sexual problems cannot be ignored. Like financial problems, they often signal an underlying issue, which if left untreated, can cause destruction in the relationship.

FOR ENGAGED COUPLES
1. Please list any questions you would like to address in your next session: _____

FOR MARRIED COUPLES:
2. Please list any questions or needs that you have in the area of your physical relationship? _____

SESSION SIX, pp. 111-137

UNGODLY SOUL TIE MINISTRY

📖 **"...For this reason a man shall leave his father and mother and be joined to his wife, and the two shall become one flesh. So then, they are no longer two but one flesh. Therefore what God has joined together, let not man separate." Matthew 19:5-6**

In order to be truly one with our spouse, we must "leave" our parents and our soul must not be tied in an ungodly way to someone else. Leaving our parents means that we continue in good relationship with them and we may value their opinions and insights, but we shift our primary, most influential human relationship to our spouse. You can read the story of an ungodly soul tie between Shechem and Dinah in Genesis 34. Dinah lived with Shechem after he raped her. This Scripture passage also demonstrates the sinfulness in the lives of those whose souls are tied to one another in an ungodly way. Instead of honoring God, their choices were influenced by their feelings toward one another. ICo. 6:16 says "...he which is joined to a harlot is one body." (One flesh) In Genesis 2:7, it says "...man became a living soul." This word "soul" also refers to a living "body". A soul tie can be a body tie or an emotional tie.

A person can actually control, manipulate, or abuse another through ungodly soul ties because the mind, will, and emotions of these two people are now open to one another. Even in seemingly good relationships, ungodly soul ties can develop if those relationships are not in divine order."[43] (e.g. lack of leaving and cleaving in marriage, previous sexual relationships, lack of order in a marriage relationship.) "Not only are the souls of persons who have been promiscuous drawn to all their former lovers, but when they marry they often have sexual and communication problems with their mates."[44] Through ministry as described in Matthew 18:18 (binding and losing), people can be set free from ungodly soul ties. It will be necessary to walk out this freedom by refusing to dwell on memories of past relationships, by living a pure lifestyle, and by keeping allegiance to Jesus and obedience to Him foremost in your desires.

When an ungodly soul tie exists, there is a significant bond between two people in which the behavior and attitudes of one person strongly influence the other in a negative way. This type of bond can occur in marriage and dating relationships, between intimate friends, with sexual partners, between parent and child, between spiritual leaders and their members, between those in authority and those submitted to them. Even healthy relationships can cross over into codependency, in which neither person feels totally free to serve the Lord. The strength of these bonds can be sufficient to cause negative pressure upon a person, even after the relationship has ended. It is also possible for people to form an ungodly tie to inanimate objects such as food, drugs, pornography, certain objects, etc. These bonds must also be broken.

If the bond from a previous dating or sexual relationship remains unbroken, if the parent has not released a son or daughter as they have become capable of being independent, if a spiritual leader has undue influence on someone's personal life, if someone experiences a longing for approval from a certain person, soul tie ministry is advised. There are also other

---

[43] **Greenwald**
[44] **Greenwald**

SESSION SIX, pp. 111-137

instances when this ministry may be recommended, such as a history of drug use with certain people, rituals and occult involvement, gambling or drinking "buddies", pornographic images that recur, first love, etc. If there has been an ungodly tie between a husband and wife (e.g. through premarital sex with each other or through a controlling relationship), they leave the godly tie in place when they pray to break the ungodly ties.

Some of the blessings of receiving ministry in this area are:

* Freedom from pressures in your life which have existed because of ties to someone who may be struggling spiritually.

* Freedom to serve the Lord with all your heart.

* Freedom to enter fully into your present relationship.

Ask the Holy Spirit to reveal any ungodly soul ties which need to be broken. (It is not necessary to remember the names of each one. The Lord knows your heart and your intentions.) See the prayer on the next page.

Prayer to break ungodly soul ties:

* Confess the soul tie. (Admit it exists.)

* Repent.

* Forgive, as necessary.

* Ask God to loose you from all ungodly soul ties and past sexual partners. Sever each ungodly soul tie, one by one. Pray that He would free you from the longings, memories, dependencies and habitual thoughts related to those relationships.

* Pray that the Lord would cleanse you and set you free … free to serve Him with all your heart … and, if you are married, free to give yourself fully to your mate.

SESSION SIX, pp. 111-137

LOVE AND PURITY

This topic is most often addressed to engaged couples, but it can be very beneficial for married couples also, as they may have established an unhealthy pattern in their relationship if they engaged in sinful sexual behavior prior to marriage.

Many couples report that maintaining their agreement or unspoken boundary in the area of sexual purity is difficult.

If you are engaged and you are doing well in this area, your respect for one another will build trust and enhance your physical relationship after marriage. According to John Fichtner,[45] "A woman instinctively knows that the toughest of all areas for a man while they are dating is the physical area." He says that "the degree that she can trust him in the physical area of their relationship (while dating) is the degree that she can trust him in" **other areas** of their relationship after they marry. If a man does not assume godly leadership in the area of physical affection while dating, the woman will be in a position of having to resist his advances. Her ability to trust will be impaired, and it's likely that this pattern will continue after marriage: the man leads, the woman resists (**not** just in areas related to their physical relationship), not trusting.

If you are married and there were difficulties in the area of impurity before marriage, this may contribute to relationship problems in the areas of trust and submission. Please see the prayer guidelines at the bottom of the page.

If you are engaged and you are struggling in the area of sexual purity, let us encourage you that it is not too late to begin a chaste relationship! In fact, it's essential that you establish this commitment to one another at this time. Real love is selfless, willing to subdue it's own desires and to care for the other person's needs in ways that build trust and please the Lord.

Don't hesitate to ask for support in this area. Pastors, home group leaders or other strong Christian friends will pray with you and help you to be accountable.

Helpful suggestions:
- Discuss this aspect of your relationship. Share your convictions with one another and set specific limits based upon the most conservative viewpoint.
- Spend time with others.
- Participate in ministry opportunities, especially those related to your vision.
- Meet in public places: parks, the library, restaurants, etc.
- Be accountable to your counselors or someone you trust.
- Avoid secluded places, especially if they have been a source of temptation in the past.
- Form the habit of praying together at the end of your times together.

Pray together now about this aspect of your relationship:
1. Ask forgiveness of each other for any part you played in difficulty in the area of purity.
2. Forgive each other.
3. Repent to God and ask His forgiveness. Commit to purity and trustworthiness.
4. Forgive yourselves.
5. Pray, as the Holy Spirit leads, for grace and for wisdom.

SIXTH JOINT SESSION, pp. 135-138

SIXTH JOINT SESSION, pp. 135-138

Prior to this session:

- Make copies of pages 113-114, 117, and 119.
- Gather all data you will need in order to prepare a budget together and to record the yearly expenses on your periodic budget form, page 119.

SIXTH JOINT SESSION

1. PRAY, asking God's direction as you undertake this very important project.
2. BEGIN by sharing with each other your preliminary versions of the five year plan.
   a. Note areas in which you agree.
   b. Note areas of ministry or activity that would be new to you.
   c. Take turns sharing as you go through each section of the plan.
   d. Go through the plans again and discern the will of the Lord as best you can, combining, eliminating, or adding ideas as He leads. Make a copy of your final version on a copy of pages 113-114 of your workbook.
   e. Your ministry is very important to the Lord! If you desire to know His will in this area, He will do all He can to clarify it for you over time. We suggest that you review and pray over your five year plan each January, giving the Holy Spirit special opportunity to revise and expand it.
3. MERGE YOUR BUDGET FORM PROPOSALS, developing a form that meets your needs.
4. FILL IN A BUDGET for the upcoming month, using a copy of page 117.
5. SEE QUESTIONS #1 AND #2 at the bottom of page 130, so these needs can be addressed at this time.
6. USING THE FEELING FORMULA, take turns sharing with each other how you feel as you think about the plans the Lord has for you.
7. TAKE THIS OPPORTUNITY to ask the Holy Spirit to reveal any areas for which you need to repent and forgive one another. Be especially sensitive to wrong attitudes, or a lack of faithfulness with the new commitments you have made as a result of this course. Remember that every time we repent, we receive grace to grow in that particular area.
8. PRAY through the Relationship Pledge on the next page now.
9. WE HOPE that this has been a profitable experience for you. If you have suggestions for us regarding this workbook, we would appreciate your input! See the back of this book for contact information.

✓ SEE PAGE 137

SIXTH JOINT SESSION, pp. 135-138

RELATIONSHIP PLEDGE

Read each point in this pledge out loud to one another. (e.g. Husband / fiancée read point one to your partner, then wife / fiancée read the same point to your partner.)

1. I will place my relationship with God before all others.
2. With God's help, to the best of my ability, I will cherish, honor, love and respect you all the days of my life.
3. I will pursue, with all my heart, the fulfillment of the purpose for which God has brought us together.
4. I will use the feeling formula often.
5. I will take responsibility for my feelings.
6. I will give good feedback when you share with me. I will be a safe place for you.
7. I will resolve conflicts regularly, using the "Do's and Don'ts".
8. I will seek to be changed more than to change you.
9. I will not take part in gossip. Our home will be a place where others are respected and confidences are kept.
10. I will trust God as He works through you to change and mature me.
11. I will make time for our relationship: time to pray, time to play, time to resolve issues and to share feelings, time for our ministry together, and (if married: time for our physical relationship and time for our family).
12. Make other pledges, as appropriate for your relationship, single or married:
    a. Purity in physical relationship: I will _____

    b. Breaking of habits: As the Lord leads, I will _____

    c. Restoration from hurts or betrayal: I will _____

14. Man: I will yield to God as He conforms me into His image as a servant leader.
15. Woman: With God's help, I will fulfill my role as your compliment, your helpmeet, your completement.
16. Both: I realize that these changes will take time and I give you permission to follow the Lord as He completes each one in you. I commit to work on myself and to entrust you to the Lord.

Signed _____ Date _____

Signed _____ Date _____

SIXTH JOINT SESSION, pp. 135-138

MARRIAGE

The Scriptures which apply to the church can also be applied to the marriage relationship. Ephesians chapter five refers to marriage, but in verse 32, Paul says that he is speaking also regarding the relationship between Christ and His bride, the Church.

So, in Philippians 2:15b-16a, when Paul talks about the stars (the Church) reflecting the light (the "sun"/ Son, Christ) to the world, it also means that a wife reflects the glory of the husband (ICo.11:7). And the glory of the husband (and therefore also the wife's) is Jesus (ICo,11:7), the light of the world. (Jn.12:46)

Therefore, when the world sees the unusual love between a godly husband and wife, they are really seeing a type of the love that that God has for His people! In this way, the marriage relationship is one of the greatest witnessing tools we have. Even without words, it is a testimony of Jesus, a light in a dark world. It can cause people to notice - and ask - and be drawn to Jesus!

You have just completed the marriage course! It has been a pleasure to meet with you at this very important time in your lives.

We will be in touch with you to schedule a follow up session during the month of _____.

If you have questions or would like support, please call (Phone: _____) or email (_____)

We care very much about the success of your marriage and the fulfillment of all that the Lord has planned for you. May the Lord bless you and hold you close. May His love be revealed to the world by the love you have for one another. You will be in our prayers!

SIXTH JOINT SESSION, pp. 135-138